EMOTIONAL SELF-REGULATION AND ARTISTIC THERAPIES

Dr. Patricia Sherwood

National Library of Australia Cataloguing-in-Publication entry

Title: Emotional Self-Regulation And Artistic Therapies
Author: Dr Sherwood, Patricia

ISBN: 978-0-9876143-5-3

Subjects: Counselling, Psychology, Art therapy
Date of Publication: March 2023.

All rights reserved. No part of this book may be reproduced in any form or by any means electronic or mechanical including, photocopying, recording or any information-storage system without written permission from the publisher.

Disclaimer

While every care has been taken in researching and compiling the information in this book, it is in no way intended to replace professional medical advice and counselling. Readers are encouraged to seek such help as they deem necessary. The author and publisher specifically disclaim any liability arising from the application of information in this book.

Layout and design by Manish Pathak

Cover picturehttps://www.traumaandbeyondcenter.com/blog/art-therapy-to-tap-into-the-unconscious-mind/

DEDICATION

To all the practitioner graduates of Sophia College who have encouraged me to write another book and especially to Tracy Cockerton, Frank and Rosemary Kroll whose care, support and positive upholding has made the writing of this book possible.

TABLE OF CONTENTS

Dedication iii

Chapter 1   Introduction to Self-Regulation and
Artistic therapies 1

Chapter 2   Situation Selection 15

Chapter 3   Situation modification 29

Chapter 4   Attentional deployment 43

Chapter 5   Cognitive change 61

Chapter 6   Response Modulation 101

Chapter 7   Conclusion 117

CHAPTER 1

INTRODUCTION TO SELF-REGULATION AND ARTISTIC THERAPIES

Ref: https://www.khaleejtimes.com/art-and-culture/heal-thyself-with

Emotional Self-Regulation and Artistic Therapies

"Expressive art therapy integrates all of the arts in a safe, non-judgmental setting to facilitate personal growth and healing. To use the arts expressively means going into our inner realms to discover feelings and to express them through visual art, movement, sound, writing or drama. This process fosters release, self-understanding, insight and awakens creativity and transpersonal states of consciousness." – Natalie Rogers

Introduction

Daniel throws a tantrum in the playground because he can't join the soccer game. In class, Matilda is crying because someone looked at her in a way she felt was hostile. Julian has pushed over a class mate who he feels has taken the building blocks that he wanted and Archie has thrown a book at the teacher who corrected his errors. Today classrooms and playgrounds as well as family homes are increasingly characterised by children who need skills to regulate their emotions. There is an epidemic of emotional dysregulation. The causes are multiple: absent parents, lack of social skill training in early childhood, over use of technology and screens which promote winning over others at any cost, exhaustion from a fast paced lifestyle, junk food, inadequate sleep, over indulgence in sugar, lack of a lifestyle that is rhythmical and predictable, and inadequate physical exercise. While the problem clearly has familial, social, economic and political roots, carers and teachers are faced with increasing demands to facilitate the development of emotional self-regulation among children in their care and there is increasing use of prescribed medications and labeling to manage many of these children with self-regulation disorders.

Emotional self-regulation is the capacity to respond to the varied, unpredictable and ongoing demands of one's environment in a way that is socially acceptable and with sufficient flexibility to enable on the spot assessment, spontaneous responses when appropriate, and deferred gratification when not appropriate (Cole et al. 1994). This capacity should increase over the lifespan, but it is helpful if identified early in problematic children. However, it needs to be pointed out that many children live in environments where parents demonstrate considerable emotional dysregulation from outright physical violence to yelling, screaming, arguing and demanding their way in controlling and disrespectful manners. Children, need modeling as their greatest learning need around emotional regulation. They need functional and healthy adult assistance to not only identify when they fail, but to develop social skills and strategies to express their needs and frustrations in positive and productive ways as well as lifestyles that are not inducing over-arousal of the nervous system. The levels of stress in children due to over-arousal has resulted in behaviors such as aggression, irritability, frustration, boredom, defiance, refusal to comply with directions, as well as a range of physical disorders including sleep difficulties, weight loss or gain, stomach aches and lowered immunity which are all conditions which increase vulnerability to emotional dysregulation (Culbert and Goelitz, accessed 2-2-2023, Rozman et al., 1994, Cole et al, 2000).

Emotional self-regulation is a complex set of skills that individuals differ in capacity to acquire. These include inhibiting, modulating, accommodating, deferring and articulating in a positive manner one's thoughts and feelings when aroused emotionally. Over regulation can result in crushing the child's spirit and creativity while under-regulation can result in social alienation, lack of friends, poor academic performance and problems in obtaining and maintaining a family and work in later life. When emotional life is simply repressed mental health is also at risk. MCraty et al (2000) in their research have also shown a clear positive correlation between academic performance and the rhythm of the heart. Unless the breathing is rhythmical the heart rhythms are disturbed and the child cannot focus adequately on cognitive tasks. Such children are prone to emotional dysregulation.

Extremes of dysregulation and repression contribute to depression, anxiety, eating disorders and addiction and emotional dysregulation (Aldao et. al 2010).In the long term, it is more skilful to actively teach social and emotional skills, strategies and mind body techniques that promote self-regulation rather than simply medicating the child to override the dysfunctional behavior. Examples include mental imagery, biofeedback, hypnosis, muscle relaxation, meditation, autogenics and the artistic therapies. (Culbert and Goelitz, accessed 2-2-2023.) The HeartMath Institute teach a range of useful tools to bring about self-regulation and these include Quick Coherence, Heart Lock, Neutral, Inner Ease and Freeze Frame which are suitable for both children and adolescents and adults as they are simple and easily achievable. These are outlined in the free resource section of the HeartMath website including the following downloadable video.https://www.heartmath.org/resources/downloads/helping-children-manage-stress-webinar/ (Accessed 2-2-2023)

The focus of this book will be upon the application of artistic therapies which has proven to be extremely effective in developing emotional self-regulation in children.

Holistic Models of Emotional Self-Regulation.

The Anthroposophical educational model of a human being is balancing thinking (cognition), feeling (heart) and willing (behaviour) sometimes referred to as the balanced integration of "heads, hearts and hands" is essential for emotional self-regulation. Rehbach (2014) elucidates further:

Dr. Patricia Sherwood

The human organism, that most complex of all natural organisms, can be described as consisting of three systems, working side by side. To a certain extent each function separately and independently of the others. One of these consists of the life of the nerves and senses. It may be named, after the part where it is more or less centered, the head organism. Second, comes what we need to recognize as another branch if we really want to understand the human organism, the rhythmic system. This includes the breathing and the circulation of the blood, everything that finds expression in rhythmic processes in the human organism. The third must be recognized as consisting of all those organs that have to do with the actual transformation of matter — the metabolic process. These three systems comprise everything that, duly coordinated, keeps the whole human complex in healthy working order.

Key to emotional self-regulation is the co-ordination or rhythmical balance between these three aspects of a child and in particular, it is the breath moving through the rhythms of the heart that produce the capacity to self-regulate. The HeartMath Institute led by Roland MCraty (2000, 2015) has produced considerable evidence showing the positive correlation between the rhythms of the heart and the capacity to perform cognitively and to self-regulate emotionally. They have produced computer games in which "coherence", or emotional self regulation is promoted and developed by the games which show them what their heart is doing and how to restore a balanced heart rhythm through their breathing. (Culbert and Goelitz, Accessed 2-2-2023). I have developed artistic processes that promote the restoration of the heart rhythms and the unlocking of contracted breathing which is at the core of poor self-regulation.

Artistic Therapies and Emotional Self-Regulation
There is growing support for the artistic therapies in emotional self-regulation. Haeyen and Noorthoom (2021) have trialed and refined the Self-Expression Emotion Regulation in Art Therapy Scale (SERATS) which was developed to monitor the specific effects of art therapy, and in particular to measure perceived effects of art therapy among patients with emotional and self-regulation problems. They concluded the SERATS scale was a positive and user friendly way to measure the effects of art therapy on emotional self-regulation:

> ….what the SERATS measures is highly associated with emotion regulation strategies like acceptance, reappraisal, discharge and problem solving and with improved sense of self including self-identity, increased self-esteem and improved agency as well as the healthy side of art making..

According to Schlenger (2021) art therapy addresses three core aspects that relate to emotional self-regulation:
 Emotional safety: A trusting therapeutic relationship can help foster a safe and non-judgmental space for expressing and processing your physical feelings.

Emotional validation: Being able to see a visual representation of your feelings and having someone witness your vulnerability in a safe way can validate your feelings.

Emotional agency: Experiencing the creative process from start to finish can help restore a sense of agency and control over your emotions and overall mental health.

Moula (2020) completed a systematic meta analysis of art therapy in schools to alleviate and prevent children's emotional difficulties which included the use of visual arts media, such as, drawing, painting, sculpture, clay, or digital art media. This systematic review aimed to summarise the results from school-based art therapy studies, and to appraise the effectiveness for children aged 5–12. Ten major electronic databases were systematically searched. In addition, journals and books were searched, and contact was made with experts in the field. The results suggested that art therapy is effective in improving children's quality of life; anxiety; self-concept; problem-solving skills, attitudes towards school; emotional and behavioural difficulties.

Nazeri et. Al (2020) examined the effect of the expressive arts on the emotional regulation of primary school children and concluded that:

> Through using self-expression, imagination, active participation, mind-body relationship and by activating and strengthening the cerebral cortex networks, expressive arts therapy can improve the positive emotion regulation skills which can help children to cope with stressful situations and to manage their behaviours.

Emotional Self-Regulation and Artistic Therapies

This book will focus on the use of artistic therapies to develop emotional regulation in children between the ages of 4 and 12 years. Many of the exercises are relevant to adolescents as well. While talking to a child and explaining appropriate responses is helpful, children learn better through concrete experiences that facilitate emotional expression such as movement, sounding, music, singing, breathing, painting, clay work and other expressive therapies such as nature therapy, equine therapy, pet therapy. Sport can also provide an excellent outlet for repressed feelings that otherwise would explode at some time. These experiences facilitate empathy development, connection, social awareness, negative emotional downloading in appropriate and socially acceptable ways. Sherwood (2013, p.3) elucidates:

> Nonverbal therapies… develop emotional literacy that is community based, child centred, family focused and culturally appropriate and that also facilitates the expression of their burgeoning inner life of experiences not previously accessed or expressed.

Emotional regulation is a central focus for school age children and as they move into concrete operational thinking, they are more able to understand concrete processes and follow them as expressed in the artistic therapies. Abstract intellectual and verbal processes are more challenging to the concrete thinker. During this age, they can come to understand socially prescribed rules and responses that are situationally determined in a way that is overwhelming for preschoolers and primary school children. They are able to follow through on artistic processes as outlined in this book. Once completed under supervision they are also not reliant on the presence of the therapist to repeat the processes if required.

Artistic therapies are diverse and manifold and a range of selections will be proffered to assist in skill training for emotional regulation. The approach is based on the Holistic Counselling model (outlined in Sherwood, 2010). Essentially it offers the child the capacity to express repressed emotions while cultivating the skills to express positive emotions through the practice of processes that provide the child with the means to express, identify, intervene and transform troublesome emotions. These processes are repeatable with groups of children or different individuals and are clearly enumerated in steps with clearly defined diagnostic, intervention and evaluation steps built into the sequences.

These interventions will be framed around the Process Model of Emotional Regulation (Gross and Thomson, 2007) who propose that emotional generation occurs in the following sequence over time;

1. Situation that is emotionally relevant to the child
2. Attention of child becomes focused upon the situation
3. Appraisal by the child of the situation based on their previous experiences and perceptions
4. Response by the child involves both behavioural and physiological dimensions.

These four stages become enmeshed in a feedback loop which can be positive or negative. Gross (1998) goes on to propose that there are 5 different points of intervention in the emotional response, each of which can lead to emotional regulation or emotional dysregulation, depending on the particular type of response. These are identified as follows:

Emotional Self-Regulation and Artistic Therapies

1. **Situation selection:**
   This involves choosing to engage or disengage from a potentially emotional encounter, and involves the ability to predict one's likely emotional response in a particular situation which is a challenging task unless one has past experience with that particular situation. Often skilful adult parents or carers will facilitate this with children such as the teacher of 6 year old children who know they will be tired and more likely to be prone to emotional dysregulation after their unusual two week swimming lessons. The teacher then lightens the need to focus cognitively when the children return from swimming lessons.

2. **Situation modification**
   This involves specifically altering one's internal or external environment to change one's perception and experienced reality. Examples include injecting humour into a situation, visualizing shrinking the trigger into a tiny dot or physically distancing oneself from the trigger.

3. **Attentional Deployment**
   This requires one to redirect one's attention away from the emotional trigger. There are many cognitive strategies for doing this and Gross (2020) identifies four. These are distraction such as disappearing into Information Technology (IT), using headphones, loud music or simply distancing from the situation as adolescents who say "whatever" when challenged. Another strategy is rumination which is repeatedly replaying the situation internally while responding passively to the situation. This is highly correlated with depression. Worry with its companion catastrophising can consume one's energy in an emotionally charged situation and prevent one from generating an appropriate response. Finally, thought suppression, which while temporary producing a relief in the long term, may lead to other maladaptive behaviours.

4. **Cognitive change**

   These are varied and frequently use and include reappraising the situation so as to reduce its emotional content and impact, distancing oneself by re-evaluating the importance of the trigger event in one's life; and humour which has been demonstrated to be a very effective emotional regulation strategy as well as socially acceptable, and at times desirable.

5. **Response Modulation**

   This involves direct attempts to influence one's behavioural, experiential and physiological response systems and may include both skilful and unskillful strategies. Skilful strategies include regular exercise, regular sleep of sufficient length and quality, avoiding sugar highs and lows by eating good food at regular intervals, swimming, massage, and for some people yoga and meditation may be effective. Negative and unskillful strategies include drug use and overuse of both prescription and recreational types of drugs.

This book will focus on practical hands on art therapy processes utilising clay, sand, colour, movement and breathing that are productive in promoting self-regulation under the five headings of the process model strategies to illustrate how artistic therapies can be used to promote emotional self-regulation. In summary these are:

1. situation selection.
2. situation modification.
3. attentional deployment.
4. cognitive change.
5. response modulation.

Upon completion of this book, persons working with children and adolescents in a counselling setting, particularly schools, should

Emotional Self-Regulation and Artistic Therapies

be better equipped with a range of innovative sequences and tools drawn from the artistic therapies of clay, colour, sand and drama which are somatically (body) based and which work effectively to increase the client's ability to regulate their emotions.

References:

Aldao, Amelia; Nolen-Hoeksema, Susan; Schweizer, Susanne (2010) "Emotion-regulation strategies across psychopathology: A meta-analytic review". *Clinical Psychology Review*. **30** (2): 217–237. doi:10.1016/j.cpr.2009.11.004. PMID 20015584.

Cole, Pamela M.; Michel, Margaret K.; Teti, Laureen O'Donnell (1994). "The Development of Emotion Regulation and Dysregulation: A Clinical Perspective". *Monographs of the Society for Research in Child Development*. **59** (2/3): 73–100. doi:10.1111/j.1540-5834.1994.tb01278.x. JSTOR 1166139. PMID 7984169.

Culbert,T. and Goelitz, J. *Helping Children Manage Stress* https://www.heartmath.org/resources/downloads/helping-children-manage-stress-webinar/

Accessed 2-2-2023.

Gross, J. J. (1998). "The emerging field of emotion regulation: An integrative review". *Review of General Psychology*. **2** (3): 271–299. CiteSeerX 10.1.1.476.7042. doi:10.1037/1089-2680.2.3.271. S2CID 6236938.

Gross, J. J. & Thompson, R. A. (2007). Emotion regulation: Conceptual foundations. In J. J. Gross (Ed.), *Handbook of Emotion Regulation* (pp. 3-24). New York: Guilford Press.

Haeyen, S and Noorthoom, E (2021) *Validity of the self-expression and emotional regulation in Art therapy scale (SERATS)* (PLoS One. 2021; 16(3): e0248315.Published online 2021 Mar 10. doi: 10.1371/journal.pone.0248315

McCraty, R. & Shaffer, F. (2015). Heart Rate Variability: New Perspectives on Physiological

Mechanisms, Assessment of Self-regulatory Capacity, and Health Risk. *Global Adv Health Med*, 4(1); 46-61.

McCraty, R., Tomasino, D., Atkinson, M., Aasen, P., &Thurik, S. (2000). *Improving test taking skills and academic performance in high school* students using Heart Math learning enhancement tools. Boulder Creek: Institute of Heart Math press.

Moula, Z., (2020) A systematic review of the effectiveness of art therapy delivered in school-based settings to children aged 5–12 years. *International Journal of Art therapy* vol 25, issue2, pp 88-99. https://doi.org/10.1080/17454832.2020.1751219

Nazeri, A., Ghamarani, A., Darouei, P., Tabatabaei, G., (2020) The Effects of Expressive arts therapy on the emotional regulation of primary school children, *Journal of Child Mental Health* 2020. vol 7, issue2, pp132-134.

HeartMath.org(2016): https://www.heartmath.org/resources/heartmath-tools/quick-coherence-technique-for-ages-12-18/

Rozman, D., McCraty, R., Goelitz, J., (2000) *The role of the Heart inLearning and Intelligence: a summary of research and applications with children*

Rehbach, Conrad (2014) *Thinking, Feeling and Willing, the threefold Human Being.* Cited 2-2-2023. https://www.sophiainstitute.us/blog/thinking-feeling-and-willing-the-threefold-human-being

Schengler(2021) https://onlinecounselingprograms.com/resources/art-therapy-young-adults/ Accessed 3-2-2023

Sherwood, P., (2010) *Holistic Counselling a New Vision for Mental Health.* Sophia Publications, Bunbury, Western Australia.

Sherwood, P., (2013) *Emotional Literacy for Adolescent Mental Health,* Acer, Melbourne.

CHAPTER 2

SITUATION SELECTION

"I found I could say things with colour and shapes that I couldn't say any other way – things I had no words for." —Georgia O'Keefe

Emotional Self-Regulation and Artistic Therapies

Introduction

Amelia has experienced bullying from a group of classmates that seem to target her when she is alone and often results in her collapsing into tears from the taunts. She has developed a number of situation selection strategies to protect herself. These include avoiding the play spaces where the bullying group "hang out" and walking quickly the other way if she sees them approaching. Another strategy is staying close to her friends in the environment where the bullies are often encountered. In this way, she avoids the confrontation which results in her breaking down emotionally. She conforms to Webb's et al. (2018) definition of situation selection:

> Situation selection involves choosing situations based on their likely emotional impact and may be less cognitively taxing or challenging to implement compared to other strategies for regulating emotion, which require people to regulate their emotions 'in the moment'…. individuals who chronically experience intense emotions or who are not particularly competent at employing other emotion regulation strategies would be especially likely to benefit from situation selection.

However, while such strategies may be helpful in the early stages of managing her emotions, she needs to develop her "internal" capacity to emotionally regulate in such situations. It is here that the artistic therapies are particularly pertinent. To elucidate this further, one needs to first understand the five nonverbal languages that precede verbal language and which govern the expression and formation of emotional life. These are the languages of the first year of life but they continue to grow throughout the lifespan, although often unrecognized and unexplored in relation to the power they have in relation to management of the emotional life. Consciousness can better access the internal storage of trauma when equipped with the nonverbal modes of expression which include sensing, gesturing, visualizing, sounding and breathing identified by Tagar (1991, 1997). Clients are able to develop these languages to understand and integrate experiences and to self regulate their emotions more effectively. The five non-verbal languages are breathing, sensing, sounding, gesturing and visualizing.

Five nonverbal languages of emotion formation and regulation

Breathing
The most fundamental expression of emotion is reflected in the breathing. Difficult experiences result in different combinations of contraction of breath because it is painful to continue breathing into these places of vibrational impact. Unless one is aware of what is happening, it is automatic to avoid the pain by reducing the breathing into the site in the physical body. These contractions in the breathing, often experienced as stress in the body or at times as pain, become a map for negative emotional experience. The shape of that spasm of not breathing captures the experience of the loss as it is imprinted in our body. That is the gesture of our pain. Literally, the physical body is an absorber of emotional experience and a carrier of the experience.

Gesturing.
Gesturing is "frozen breathing" which represents, through body language, the emotional state of a person. It is literally the external mirror of inner experience and can be captured in a variety of artistic mediums including clay, dance and drama. It is the primary reflector

and expresser of the body's emotional experience to the world around. Every human experience can be directly expressed in a gesture which reflects how we constrain the breathing when confronted with particular experiences which are conveyed vibrationally to the body. For example, we hear sudden news of the loss of someone we love, and we experience it in the heart. For a moment we feel a contraction in our heart, we may bow our heads, clutch parts of our body, and shake our heads in disbelief, to name just a few of the emotions that might be expressed in bodily gestures. Persons who have difficulty in situation selection and self-regulation are also frequently poor readers of the non verbal language of gesturing and the meanings of facial gestures in those around them.

Visualising.
Visualising is the inherent ability to create accurate pictures of one's inner experience. This is not guided imagery but authentic, spontaneous, visualising using one's imagination or image creating faculties. This capacity varies considerably among people and more so than any of the other languages. Usually, persons who have developed strong visualising capacities have strong appreciation of colour and have experienced childhoods in which creative play was encouraged. The capacity to use colour to express feelings often reflects one visualising capacity but more importantly the range of one's emotional expression and the scope of emotional awareness. It is interesting that one of the characteristics of many children on the autistic spectrum is the inability to draw pictures in colour. Even when given a choice the picture is usually drawn in monochrome, most often aqua blue or grey. Childhoods in which the imaginative creative capacities of image making are encouraged, enable the child to more readily express feeling and read the range of feelings in their external environment. This also facilitates situational selection and in turn capacity for emotional self-regulation.

Sounding.

The sounds of human speech, consonants and vowels, become patterns of vibrations which can resound within the body. Every sound will create an echo within a particular range of human experience. Experience, which lives in patterns of resonance, can be precisely matched with the resonance patterns of the sounds of speech and these sounds can access all levels and periods of one's life. Every human experience expressed in a gesture, can find its precise counterpart in a particular combination of sounds of speech. However, this non-verbal language is differentially developed among people. Quite often persons high on visualising languages might be less strong on sounding and vice-versa. Many traumatic experiences are triggered by particular sound patterns stored in the physical body. Awareness of these triggers facilitates self-regulation of emotions, and a child with such awareness can more readily make a situation selection, to avoid particular situations which stimulate emotional flooding or dysregulation. Children with sensory processing disorders relating to hearing must be trained to be particularly vigilant in selecting and/or avoiding situations which they experience as flooding their hearing with sounds which lead to self-regulation breakdown.

Sensing.

This is the cumulative ability of all the nonverbal languages and the senses to "read" an unwritten situation. In modern parlance one is "picking up the vibes". Sensing can be internal or external, that is one may sense inwardly as to how one is feeling, is one tired, thirsty, anger, sad, feeling empty, hungry, lonely or outward as to how another person is feeling. One may also sense environmental variables such as danger, temperature, safety and incoming weather conditions. This human ability to become aware of a phenomenon based on the cumulative activity of the senses Tagar(1997) terms "sense-ability". Through sensing, our internal experiences can be accessed, and brought once again to consciousness. Our external sensing gives us information about others. We sense for example, whether our children are heading for a sickness, whether our friends are "bursting with energy" or "looking thin". Most importantly, sensing enables one to self-regulate emotions by quickly giving information about an environment that we are about to enter. For example, when one has developed sensing, one can read a hostile intention from a group of people when directed towards oneself or others and make the appropriate choice in terms of situation selection that promotes self-care and emotional regulation.

The question remains as to why some children seem unable to sense a threatening situation and make the appropriate situation selection. They fail to read the hostile intentions of others directed towards them until they are a victim and enmeshed in the aggression. These children are often dissociated in some way either living life by disappearing into their own world or by not being present in the moment which Tagar (1997) terms "excarnation". In reality, this means that they fail to sense the obvious signs around them in the external environment or in the gestures, thoughts and potential actions of others. For example, Katey was sitting on the front fence of her home waiting for her Dad to come home from work when a man approached her wearing a raincoat which he opened in front of her and "flashed his genitals". The moment the man approached her Katey had already sprung to her feet and run quickly inside to tell her parents. She did not remain passively sitting on the fence as she sensed something was amiss with this person approaching her. This is the quality of situation selection that needs to be reactivated in those children currently dissociated who are often numb and distanced from self-awareness and sensory experience.

With the use of these tools of nonverbal communication, a child can uncover and heal undigested experience stored in vibrational patterns of sound, colour, gesture and contracted breathing, clear trauma and recreate self-awareness of the bodily sensations. In this way the child is able to sense into situations and make skilful choices on whether or not to act on them, or in some instances how to encounter them so as to avoid emotional dysregulation.

First aid drama therapy techniques to facilitate the capacity for situation selection in a child.

Identifying in one's body that one is not present.
The highest part of the mind of children, their insight, which underlies self-awareness and enables skilful situation selection, leaves their body when they are in fear, anger, grief or simply "not there" and day dreaming. So, for example, the child's physical body is in the classroom, their eyes are open, and they may even talk to you, but they are not present and cannot remember what has been said to them. Children may do this when they are bored, tired or simply unmotivated to learn something. Almost all children will do so when they feel unsafe or angry. Children do this in stages.

1. Shaking legs or feet as the breath leaves the lower part of the body first.
2. Need to go to the toilet when breath is withdrawn up to abdomen.
3. Breath is contracted up to the stomach and children will say they have "butterflies in the stomach" or feel like vomiting or have a stomach ache.
4. When the breath is contracted in the throat, the person often feels panicky and says they cannot breathe properly or may even have a panic attack.
5. When the breath is so constricted that it is contracted through the forehead, the person feels dizzy.
6. Breath rapidly leaves the body out through the crown of the head in a sudden shock and then fainting may occur.

Staying present in your body: grounding

Staying present in your body means that the child is fully present and not planning to run away or fight but to assess the situation facing them skillfully. The art therapy technique for doing this is called "grounding". The exercise of grounding is applicable to children in states of anger or fear to return them to calmness and to fully breathe again in their body.

Instructions: (for the child)

Step 1: Notice that you are angry or frightened or just simply "not focused on your work" and where in your body you feel these feelings.
Step 2: Stamp both feet on the ground and walk around the room saying out loud in unison with the steps of your feet:

"I am here, I am safe, I am protected."

Step 3: Keep repeating until you feel calm again.
Step 4: If you have a drum, you can beat it in unison with your steps as you walk and this accelerates grounding as does clapping your hands while stamping your feet.

First aid breathing techniques using colour to facilitate the capacity for situation selection in a child.

Sensing into anger or fear arising in your body

In order to make a skilful situation selection decision, the child first needs to know the early warning signs of anger or fear arising in their body. It is detecting the orange traffic light before they hit the red light and are flooded by fear or anger.

Instructions: (for the child)
Step 1: Stand up and practice breathing down to your toes.
Step 2: Breathe down to the tips of your toes until you can imagine your breath coming out of the tips of your toes.
Step 3: Sense where in the body you feel stressed or tense. It will feel uncomfortable in that part of your body.
Step 4: Place your hand on that part of your body where the tension feels strongest.
Step 5: Draw this uncomfortable feeling with your crayons on white paper. Is it like a knot, a black lump of stone, is it like a ball of string? Alternatively, you could make the shape of the feeling in clay.
Step 6: This is the shape of how you are not breathing when you are feeling scared or angry. Once you feel uncomfortable in your body it you know that you are getting either scared or angry. This happens before you get angry or scared on the outside.
Step 7: You know it is anger because you will feel hot inside and want to yell or throw something. You know it is fear because you will feel cold and shaky in your body or you will want to or hide or run away.
Step 8: once you can see how you are feeling inside you need to walk away from the situation that has left you feeling that way.

Exiting anger or fear (dysregulation)
It is important for the child to know how to exit stress, whether it is anger or fear, so that they can breathe rhythmically again and think clearly and so make good decisions regarding the situation.
Instructions: (for the child)
Step 1: Stand up and close your eyes and breathe down to your toes.
Step 2: Place your hand on the part of your body that feels uncomfortable, tense, bad or yucky.
Step 3: Collect the tense or yucky feeling into a ball with your hands and throw it away against the wall. As you throw it away say

loudly "g". Make sure it is a loud exploded 'g' like a ball bouncing off a wall.
Step 4: Take a step backwards and stamp your feet.
Step 5: Shake off the yucky/angry feeling by shaking both hands vigorously.
Step 6: Repeat steps 2-5, three to five times until you are making clear sounds of "g" against the wall, and you can feel that you are breathing fully again. Each time take a bigger step backwards.

First aid sensing techniques to facilitate the capacity for situation selection in a child.

Many children who have poor emotional self-regulation have poor sensing. They do not read the "vibes" of the situation at all or very poorly. Their capacity to sense outwardly and read others is very poor and this is often the case with children on the autistic spectrum as well. They are not very aware of how they feel inside themselves and at times they are overwhelmed by having little capacity to distinguish how others are feeling.

Sensing into smells

This simple activity which embraces colour and sensing requires the child to collect three flowers or leaves from nature that have a smell and then on three different sheets of paper sense how the smell of each item is attacking their nose. They need to draw the shape of how they experience, for example, whether it is of round droplets, or sharp needle like shapes.

Explain to the child that in all situations they need to sense out into what the energy is like, just like they were sensing out to the smell coming from the flowers or leaves. Some situations are spiky and should be avoided, while other situations are soft and warm and welcoming and it is safe to join them.

Boundary maintenance

Often the child that has difficulty grounding and being present also has poor boundaries and finds they are unable to hold their personal space and are easily overwhelmed by others.

The simplest way of creating boundaries is the following exercise based on sounding, colour, visualising and sensing.

Building the safety dome

Step 1: Stand up and stretch out your arms to feel your personal space.

Step 2: Visualise that you are standing in the middle of this safety dome and you are now creating the edges of the dome

Step 3: Choose the product out of which you wish to create the dome. It has to be strong, for example, such a brick, steel, bullet proof glass, concrete.

Step 4: Now gradually create the dome from the ground upwards by saying "d,d,d,d,d," repeatedly as you move your hands up towards the top and all around you as if creating the safe space brick by brick.

Step 5: Now draw yourself surrounded by the safety dome you have created.

Step 6: Every day create the safety dome by saying d,d,d,d out loud with the accompanying actions.

Step 7: When in a situation in which the child feels uncomfortable, recreate the dome and say the d, d, d in your head so you may remain calm and present and make a good decision on how to manage the situation.

The Eleven directions

This is another basic drama therapy exercise to strengthen a child's personal space while also grounding them. Both of these aspects assist the child to be present and hence make situational selection more easily.

Instructions (for the child)
Step 1: Stand up straight and stamp your feet in unison with what you are saying
Step 2: repeat out loud your name as you make the following gestures:
Joan above (both hands stretched out above her head).
Joan below (both hands stretched out towards her feet).
Joan to the front (both hands stretched in front of her body).
Joan to the back (both hands stretched out behind her body).
Joan to the sides (one hand stretched out on each side of her body).
And Joan within (both hands to the heart while stamping the feet in unison.

Repeat all of the above at least 3 times accompanied by each of the gestures.

At the end of the exercise ask the children to sense themselves again. Do they feel the same, stronger or weaker after this exercise? Are they breathing more fully so that they are more present. Discuss the differences that they feel in their body before and after completing the exercise.

Conclusion
It is evident that art therapy exercises particularly those drawn from drama therapy and colour which engage the nonverbal senses of breathing, sensing, gesturing, visualizing and sounding, can produce very effective sensory based training exercises. These increase the child's capacity to make skilful situation selection decisions and so support the child's capacity to maintain emotional self-regulation through bodily self-awareness and bodily self-management

References

Webb, T., Lindquist, K., Jones, K., Avishai,A., Sheeran, P., (2018) Situation selection is a particularly effective emotion regulation strategy for people who need help regulating their emotions.l*Cognitive Emotion Journal* March; 32(2):231-248.doi: 10.1080/02699931.2017.1295922. Epub 2017 Mar 1. Accessed 5-2-2023

Tagar, Y (1991) "The Use of Non-Verbal Expression in Stress management with philophonetics counselling" Gawler, 1 (ed) *Medicine of the Mind*Gawler, The Gawler Foundation, Melbourne,1999: 246-266.

Tagar, Y (1997) "Co-operating with the Life forces Within" Gawler, 1 (ed) *Medicine of the Mind,*Mind Immunity and Health Conference, Gawler Foundation, Lorne.

CHAPTER 3

SITUATION MODIFICATION

Ref: https://www.manningham.vic.gov.au/events/respect-art-therapy

Emotional Self-Regulation and Artistic Therapies

"Art is my cure to all this madness, sadness and loss of belonging in the world & through it I'll walk myself home."
— **Nikki Rowe**

Introduction:

Situation modification refers to the capacity to sense the energy of the situation and its threatening configurations and to modify it, so as to manage its emotional impact upon oneself particularly by altering the external factors. (Gross, 1998). This is a core capacity in emotional self-regulation. However, to do this one must think logically and rationally about the situation and this capacity is impeded in children who have suffered various types of trauma. Trauma activates the right side of the cortex, where the emotions are stored and deactivates the left hemisphere or rational, articulate side of the brain. As Van De Kolk (2015, p.45) notes:

> Deactivation of the left hemisphere has a direct impact on the capacity to organize experience into logical sequences and to translate our shifting feelings and perceptions in words…without sequencing we can't identify cause and effect, grasp the long-term effects of our actions, or create coherent plans for the future.

Hence, it becomes critical to recognize that children that have difficulties with emotional self-regulation, frequently have a history of trauma that impedes their ability in emotional selection situations, where the emotional brain discounts the rational left hemisphere.

In addition, the speaking part of the brain is paralyzed which is why talk therapy with such children is often useless. The benefit of art therapy is that it enables communication with the right side of the brain, enabling traumatic material to be processed, expressed and transformed and hence liberates the child to make skilful decisions from their frontal lobe. This is sometimes referred to as exercising effectively the "executive function of the brain". Only then can a child engage in situation modification.

Because trauma affects the whole body, mind and brain, and when severe and characterized by Post Traumatic Stress Disorder (PTSD), the body continues to defend against a threat that belongs to the past without being able to switch off the stress response and assess the present situation before them. Van De Kolk, (2015, p.59) refers to the triune brain where the reptilian brain stem which develops during pregnancy is basically focused on survival. The limbic brain which develops in the first 6 years is focused upon emotional relevance, categorization and perception and early trauma affects its functioning throughout life. The prefrontal cortex which is the sophisticated driver of planning, anticipation, emotional self-regulation and empathy develops last and is profoundly inhibited by early trauma exposure.

Furthermore, the emotional brain which embraces the thalamus, and the amygdala. These are the sentinels of the human being and interpret incoming emotional experience, before the prefrontal cortex or conscious reasoning, and control the child's response if the sensory input is similar to previous traumas. This prevents the child from engaging in situation modification because they fail to determine whether the situation is dangerous or safe.

There are two pathways of changing the threat detection system in the human brain that has been wrongly wired and need rewiring to engage in effective situation modification. Van De Kolk (2015, p.63) describes these:

Emotional Self-Regulation and Artistic Therapies

> ...from the top down, via modulating messages from the medial prefrontal cortex (not just the pre-frontal cortex) or from the bottom up, via the reptilian brain, through breathing, movement, touch.

I would add visualising and sensing using movement and breathing to the second pathway which points to the immense relevance of the artistic therapies in transforming trauma histories in children prone to emotional dysregulation.

There is a third pathway of course and that is the increasingly popular medication of children who demonstrate emotional dysregulation. In particular, highly traumatized children usually in foster care, are increasingly medicated. For example, 12.4 % of children in foster care in the USA are medicated compared with 1.4 % of the other children in the population (Van De Kolk, 2015,p.37). Unfortunately, while medication may subdue children's dysregulatory behaviours and make them more compliant and manageable, the personal costs are high. It reduces their natural spontaneity, creativity and individual personality as well as the extensive side effects of all of the medications including with growth issues, sleeping issues, neurological and digestive disturbances. These quick fix solutions also ignore the basic traumas underlying the emotional dysregulation, which are bound to recur in adulthood. If unaddressed they will lead to a range of problems particularly in relation to addiction, violence, depression, suicide attempts and self-harm.

Hence, it behooves us for the sake of the future of society and the individual, to work to facilitate the processing of trauma in children, so they can become functional self-fulfilled and emotionally stable adult members of society.

Art therapy interventions to promote situation selection

The following artistic therapies are a sample selection of what is available to assist in releasing, identifying and transforming trauma so that the child may increase its capacity for emotional self-regulation and situation selection in particular. However, most of these exercises which are based on the body-heart-brain connections and rhythm are also relevant to other emotional self-regulation strategies listed above. Because the arts are holistic and address the child as a whole, not just cognitively, many of the sequences outlined in this book will have multiple applications for achieving a number of the emotional regulation strategies simultaneously. These art therapy exercises assist in achieving these goals as well facilitating the development of greater social awareness.

Sand tray orientation.

A sand tray is a tactile experience involving sensing, gesturing, visualizing, colour awareness and at times sound, in which the child is able to express traumatic experience that otherwise remain repressed, hidden, ignored and denied in the left hemisphere of the brain and prevent the child from having insight to engage in situation modification.

For those not familiar with sand tray the preparatory materials are listed below

- The tray should be approximately 75cm long by 55cm wide by 15cm deep. ideally wooden or plastic with a blue base that can represent water. White or yellow sand is usually used to fill it.
- A selection of toys that represent good and bad feelings. For example:

Emotional Self-Regulation and Artistic Therapies

Mineral	Volcanoes, gems, crystals, rocks, mountains, waterfalls.
Plant	Forests, trees, roses, flowers, fruits, cactus.
Animal	Tigers, lions. Snakes, birds, butterflies, spiders, dinosaurs, sharks, dolphins, dogs, cats, lizards, elephants, monkeys, rabbits, frogs, fish, eagles, bees, bugs, horses, sheep, giraffes.
Human	Children, babies, adults, male and female. Soldiers, warriors, old and young persons, fat and thin people, Indians, black persons, clowns, sad and happy persons, mothers, fathers.
Archetypal	Wizards, fairies, angels, Buddha, Jesus, Mary, cross, star, crescent, magic wand, baddies, goodies, super heroes, shining stones/jewellery, hearts.
Mechanical	Cars, bridges, house, building, castle, fences, boats, planes, containers, food, mirrors, beds, paper money, food, skeletons, robots, clocks.

Step 1: Make the situation that you are facing in the sand tray and choose figurines to represent your feelings.

Step 2: Tell the story that you have made in the sand play,

Step 3: Identify goodies and baddies,

Step 4: Choose which piece would you like to be,

Step 5: When you have finished think what new pieces you could add to the sand play to make you feel more peaceful in the situation and add that piece

Step 6: Build fences/boundaries around any threatening pieces,

Step 7: Choose the piece that makes you feel strong and confident when facing that situation and keep it in your pocket when you have to go into that situation and remember that you have the power to change the situation,

Step 8: If you have a phone, take a photo of the final sand tray that you have made and look at it daily.

Enter-exit-behold
This drama therapy intervention enables the child to see how they could change the situation which they find overwhelming.

Step 1
Sense in your body where you feel the fear or stress when you think of the situation.
Imagine stepping into that part of your body and make the shape of the tension with your hand.

Step 2:
Draw the shape of the tension.
Imagine squeezing your whole body into that shape while holding that shape with your hands.

Step 3:
When did you feel like this before in your life?
How old where you when you felt like this before in your life?

Step 4:
Take the hand of your child self, for example the 4 or 5 or 6 year old, that felt like you feel today when you think about the stressful situation.
Tell them that they are safe and protected as you are looking after them now.

Step 5:
Draw a protective dome around this child and repeat while walking around the room holding their hand while saying "we are safe and protected".

Step 6:
In the trigger situation hold onto the hand of the fearful part of yourself that you have found. Keep telling that part: "You are safe and

protected". Breathe deeply while saying this to this part of yourself and notice the stress in the situation reduce.

Developing a guard: protecting oneself from fear in an experienced threatening situation.

This art therapy intervention using clay enables the child to modify the situation internally by creating a guard that protects them from the perceived threat. They then take the guard with them into the situation. This defuses the level of stress, otherwise experienced in that threatening situation.

Step 1: the site of the fear
Where in the body do you feel the fear when you think of the situation
Make the shape of the fear in your body in clay

Step 2: the force of the fear
Make in clay the shape of how the fear is attacking you. For example, is it like arrows, stones, and a steam roller.

Step 3: the guard that can protect them from the fear
Make a powerful image in clay that can protect you from the attacking force you have made above, for example, a big warrior, a powerful angel, a thick shield, a strong lion, or something else.
Place the clay image between you and the force of the fear that is attacking you. Now that you are protected stand up and feel your safety as you stand with the clay piece which is front of you. It protects you from the fear of the previously perceived attacking force.

Step 4: the courageous one who can face of the fear.
Make yourself in clay showing how you can stand up strongly and not be overcome by the fear now that you have a guard who protects you.

Step 5: find a sound for the guard
Think of a strong earth sound for your guard, for example,"b,b,b,b" or "d,d,d" or "g,g,g" and say it out loud daily and in your head when in the situation that you previously found threatening.

Step 6: follow up
Keep this clay image as the one that can protect you to remind you that you can call on protection when you feel you are in a situation of overwhelm. It is a way to modify the situation so you feel in control.

Speaking up
Situation modification can be affected by speaking up. Humour, asking a reflective question or Socratic style questioning (providing evidence and reasons) can all modify a situation. In addition, speaking up for one's needs can also change the direction of a situation that otherwise could be experienced as overwhelming. It moves the locus of power and control back to the person speaking up. This sequence is also completed using clay.

Step 1: To express the shape of the block
Recall the situation in which you did not speak up for your needs and how frustrated you felt. Recall the person you needed to speak up to and what you needed to say but did not and just resorted to an angry outburst or a defeated sulk. Find the part of the body that feels most uncomfortable when you recall the situation.

Step 2: finding the contracted breathing
Step into that part of the body and sense how the breath/energy is not moving or stuck in that part of the body. Is it like a ball of rock, of string, a twisted rope, a hole or something else?

Exit or step backwards then gesture the shape of the blocked energy you experienced in the above step.

Make the shape of the blocked energy in clay

Step 3: to make a tool to break through the block
Imagine what tool would be needed to break through the block.

If the block is made out of wood you might need an axe or a saw. If it is made out of metal you might need a blow torch, for example.

Make the tool to break through the block in clay

Emotional Self-Regulation and Artistic Therapies

Step 4: breaking through the block

Apply the tool to the block using a sound and gesture of the tool.

Repeat the sound and gesture of the tool until you experience that the block has been broken through.

Make in clay the shape of the block that has been broken through.

Step 5: speaking up

Speak up to the person or situation through rehearsal with the Counsellor. Speak out loud or write it down on paper then speak it out loud.

Repeat this until you can sense the power of speaking up for what you really need in that situation.

Sense how the situation changes when you imagine yourself speaking up for your needs.

Step 6: follow up

Practice speaking up prior to re-entering the situation.

In the situation speak up at the appropriate time and observe how this changes the situation compared to when you get angry or sulk in that situation.

Breathing in the rainbow

When a child is fearful of a situation, they usually experience the feeling shrinking into a smaller size which increases their tendency to fail to emotionally self-regulate because they are not present in the particular situation and perceive themselves as small, overwhelmed or unable to cope. The rainbow exercise is a way of filling the entire situation with the colours of the rainbow that emanate from your heart so that you feel that you are more in control and more able to experience the situation positively.

Step 1:

Imagine you are breathing a rainbow full of energy into every part of your body until your body is full of rainbow energy and it floods out through your fingertips and toes and fills up your personal space. Breathe this rainbow in for about 5 minutes one colour at a time until you feel full of the whole seven colours of the rainbow.

Now draw yourself using crayons or paint using all of the seven colours.

Step 2:
Keep doing this while stamping your feet. Gesture the movement of the rainbow energy through your body as you are breathing and walking around the room. Find a sound for it.

Step 3:
Now visualize the rainbow spreading out from you filling all around you and gradually moving into the whole room. It is becoming so large that it is filling the whole situation that you were previously stressed about.

See the rainbow bringing peace and happiness into that stressful situation.

Draw the rainbow surrounding everybody in the stressful situation and all the spaces within them and around them.

Step 4:
Practice this daily and remember to breathe in the rainbow and spread it through the whole situation when you are next exposed to it.

Remember that you are safe and protected by the rainbow and that you can fill the whole space with the rainbows seven colours.

Rehearsal

This is an essential part of all of the above techniques to ensure situation modification. It is critically important that the child has the opportunity to practice the techniques in front of the counsellor prior to encountering the actual situation. Rehearsal has a number of critical strengths which include increasing the child's confidence, strengthening their ego and their speaking up, promoting higher levels of self-esteem, empowering the child to understand and internalize new ways of handling a stressful situation, and opening up the opportunity for coaching and feedback from a sympathetic and supportive adult.

Conclusion

Situation modification can greatly increase positive enhancement by the above exercises drawn from the artistic therapies. They enable the child to modify the situation through bringing additional positive resources into the stressful situation and to practice speaking up in the situation. Essential to their success of course is rehearsal of the situation that has been modified. This gives the child back a sense of power and control over it.

References

Gross, J. J. (1998). "The emerging field of emotion regulation: An integrative review". *Review of General Psychology*. 2 (3): 271–299. CiteSeerX 10.1.1.476.7042. doi:10.1037/1089-2680.2.3.271. S2CID 6236938.

Van De Kolk, B., (2015) *The Body Keeps the Score*, Penguin, London

CHAPTER 4

ATTENTIONAL DEPLOYMENT

Ref: https://www.vlinderexpressiveartstherapy.com/how-is-art-therapy-remedial/

Emotional Self-Regulation and Artistic Therapies

"Art therapy encourages individuals to express and understand emotions, resolve issues and improve self-awareness. To express one's self artistically can aid in the healing process by surfacing meaning. Through art there is an opportunity to connect with the unconscious which can foster increased self-awareness. Through this connection lived experience can be explored, including both positive and negative effects enabling the opportunity for healing."
— Laurie Ponsford-Hill, The Art of Self-Supervision: Studying the Link Between Self-Reflection and Self-Care

Introduction

Attentional deployment is defined by Freer and Hajcak (2015) as:

> .... an emotion regulation strategy that involves shifting attentional focus within an emotional scene in order to modulate emotional experience. Attentional deployment is widely used and effective at reducing negative affect...

This may involve shifting attention away from the situation through strategies like distraction, thought suppression, or directing attention towards the situation with strategies like rumination, worry, and anxiety. Bebko (2014, et al.) argue that their research demonstrates that looking towards, rather than away, from an emotional situation increases the person's capcity to emotionally self-regulate.

Critically, irrespective of emotion regulation strategy, participants who looked toward emotional areas of a complex visual scene were more likely to experience emotion regulation success. Taken together, these results demonstrate that attentional deployment varies across emotion regulation strategies and that successful emotion regulation depends on the extent to which people look toward emotional content in complex visual scenes.

Essentially, attentional deployment involves shifting attention to different aspects of the situation in an attempt to emotionally self-regulate, generally restricting or narrowing the complexities of the situation into a narrow frame. This may involve distraction which involves directing attention away from the situation and focusing instead on other content, and this is common when individuals face situations of high emotional intensity. Distraction minimizes or filters out the emotional content. An example is during a serious car accident a person focuses not on the injuries, but on obtaining help or focuses their attention on their dog or the wildflowers around the car accident scene.

In rumination, a person repeatedly re-runs the situation elaborating on it and becoming so self consumed by it that they may end up with depression or PTSD. This strategy exacerbates their emotional distress and intensifies the emotional content of the situation often out of all proportion. It colours the present moment even when the person is nowhere near the stressful situation.

Worry and anxiety are other examples of attentional deployment which involve the person frequently revisiting the situation and focusing on how to solve the problem, and risking becoming flooded by the situation through feelings of powerlessness and overwhelm. When this happens, anxiety disorders may develop so that the emotional dysregulation goes beyond the situation and takes over other aspects of the person's life.

Finally, thought suppression or redirecting negative images and thoughts towards positive imagery, can provide temporary relief and increase emotional self-regulation. An example is pairing positive thoughts with negative thoughts to redirect attention onto the positive aspects of their lives. However, thought suppression may in the long term, if repeated over the same issue, result in secondary manifestation such as obsessive compulsive thoughts (Lowenstein, 2007).

To understand more deeply the strategy of attentional deployment which can exacerbate mental health in the intermediate and long term, it is necessary to understand the biological foundations for survival that are switched on under emotional pressure. The thalamus which is normally the central component of attention and concentration breaks down during trauma. Memory is often a string of isolated sensory imprints, and physical sensations accompanied by helplessness without any rational or logical progression. During intense trauma the right and left prefrontal cortex are deactivated. People lose the sense of time and space and become trapped in the moment of terror and fear. Dissociation or blanking out is one strategy for survival which restricts thinking, focus and emotion. Here the person blanks out reality and focuses on something not in the present moment often in a surrealistic world. They may then suffer from depersonalization or inability to feel anything and so miss out on the joy of life. Another strategy is rumination over the traumatic event. Van De Kolk, (2015, p.73-) describes this attentional deployment underlying PTSD:

> One of the reasons that traumatic memories become dominant in PTSD is that it's so difficult to feel truly alive right now when you can't be fully here, you go to places where you did feel alive –even if these places are filled with horror and misery.

Van De Kolk proposes that desensitization as a therapy strategy is unhelpful because although it may increase emotional self-regulation, it disconnects the client from the satisfaction of daily experiences. He argues for strengthening their experiences in the present moment, and advocates sensory based positive experiences such as art therapy, equine therapies, wilderness, therapies, and drama therapies, that strengthen engagement of the brain in the pleasures of the present moment. In essence, solutions must involve helping the person who is traumatized to alter the inner sensory landscape of their bodies, so they can engage in the positive experiences of nurture, love, care, connectedness, safe people and nurturing places.

> For us humans, it means that as long as the mind is defending against invisible assaults our closest bonds are threatened, along with our ability to imagine, plan, play learn and pay attention to other people's needs. (Van De Kolk, 2015, p.76).

Not surprising then those self-regulation strategies like distraction which frequently involves addiction, cutting and other dysfunctional experiences to avoid facing the emotional stimulus and its underlying trauma, are very common among adolescents. Self-regulation moves to focus upon experiences that filter out any high intensity emotional content that has not been integrated into their experience and consequently is experienced as unpleasant and overwhelming. In addition, rumination which frequently leads down a negative spiral resulting in depression. There is loss of purpose and consequent action which involves both movement and engagement in emotions and which Pavlov saw as the most important qualities of life. These are needed to be organized to enhance one's life rather that suppressed or extinguished. (cited in Van De Kolk, 2015, p.78).

The Ventral Vagal complex (VCC)

In order to contextualise the attentional deployment strategies for emotional self-regulation, it is necessary to to understand thebody-mind-emotion connection which is governed by the Vagus . When it runs the show we smile when others welcome us and react with anger or fear when rejected or criticised. It sends signals to the heart, lungs and gut. When we are traumatised the vagus nerve engages the sympathetic nervous system and our voice becomes faster, our pitch intensifies, our heart races and often we sweat or start to shake uncontrollably. This triggers the fight/flight reaction. The fight reaction is seen as emotional dysregulation and is most apparent in children who are subject to threatening and hostile conditions in the homes. While this is not desirable it is preferable to the freeze reaction in which the child disappears, and is unreachable. Self and other awareness is shut off, the heart slows down, there may be nausea or diarrhea and often there is no reaction to external events because the child is fully dissociated. They may fail to register any physical pain, have memory loss and may focus on irrelevant stimuli to deploy attention away from the area. This is the most serious type of trauma response and although the child using this type of attentional deployment may be easier to manage than the child who is in fight mode and whose emotional self-regulation has collapsed into shouting, kicking, biting, throwing chairs or other objects, the former reaction of disappearance should be of greater concern in the long term, than the emotional self-dysregulation of the child in freeze mode.

Positive rhythmical self-engagment in the present moment is essential to both of these types of dysregulation and this can most readily be achieved through physical movement, the creative arts , drama and any activity that restores the breathing rhythm and the joy of being in the present moment. Cognitive reasoning is often least effective:

> ... many methods that profess to treat trauma tend to bypass this emotional engagement system and instead focus on recruiting the cognitive capacities of themind. Despite the well documented effects of anger, fear and anxiety on the ability to reason many programs continue to ignore the need to engage the safety system of the brain.. the last thing that should be cut from the school schedules are the chorus, phsyical education, recess and anything else involving movement, play and joyful engagement. (Van De Kolk, 2015, p. 88).

Hence the following processes and sequences drawn from the artistic therapies address these basic needs to restore the rhythmn and breathing within the physical body, so that the mind may become receptive to learning and cognitive strategies that may further facilitate the management of emotions.

Resourcing for abandonment and rejection

This exercise deflects attention away from rumination on the experience of being rejected and re-mobilises the child's body through sound, gesture and movement. One needs to find new ways of bringing joy and connectedness into their bodies, hearts and minds.

Step 1:
Identify which part of your body feels most empty, sad or abandoned.

Step 2:
Name what is missing from this part of your body in terms of qualities: joy, love, warmth, fun, connection, and friends.

Step 3
Choose the missing quality you need most.

Step 4
Choose someone who has lots of this quality or some other person or animal that you know who has this quality in abundance.
Imagine receiving this quality from that person as if it was raining upon you and around you. Drink it in and breathe deeply while you are drinking in that quality.

Step 5
Breathe in that quality into the part of the body that is empty or sad or disappointed.

Step 6
Choose a colour for that quality and breathe in that colour and wrap a scarf of that colour around yourself.

Step 7
Walk in the bodily gesture of the new quality so you can feel how your body is a different shape compared to when you feel empty and disappointed.

Step 8
Make the sound of that quality or choose a song that contains that quality and listen to it.

Step 9
Draw yourself full of this good quality using crayons or paint the colours that you can now breathe through your body.

Step 10
Question yourself on how can you bring more of that quality into yourself? What activities could you engage in that would increase your happiness and joy in the world: examples are horse riding, loving a dog or cat, going camping in the wilderness, joining a team sport.

Enlarging the light and hope in the face of stress and dysregulation

This artistic exercise uses distraction but in a positive way to move the child from the feeling of distress into a feeling of positivity. It teaches the child to find a doorway to escape from stressful situations in which they are prone to emotional dysregulation. It will remind them of bodily experiences of calm and contentment.

Step 1:
Paint or draw the colours of your sadness. Just the shapes and colours. You don't need to draw a picture.
Look for the lightest colour in the drawing: yellow, or light blue, or light green, or pink; even if they are covered over by black and brown

Step 2:
With your "X ray eyes" look at what is inside that light colour in your drawing even if it is only a little dot.
Draw what is inside the light colour. It will be a picture of something you like and helps you to feel happier in your life.

Step 3:
Keep this last picture and photograph it on your phone if you have one.

Emotional Self-Regulation and Artistic Therapies

When in the challenging situation where you feel threatened or abandoned, focus on this place of joy for your self whether it be the beach, your back garden, a holiday spot, or one of your favourite places to visit.

Removing betraying words and actions from your body

Instead of suppressing the feeling of betrayal, the child learns to actively sense into their body and find where they feel the betrayal and to literally with their hands imagine pulling it out. They then throw the betraying energy away, vocally expelling it by a loud 'g' sound. This also establishes the capacity to breath fully again and so return to emotional selfregulation .

Step 1: Place your hand on the part of your body where you feel the betraying energy has entered into your personal space.

Step 2: Sense whether the betrayal feels like a dagger in the back, a knife in the heart, a twisted knot in your stomach, or something else.

Step 3: Pull out the betraying energy with your hands making sounds from closed to open, such as from a consonant to a vowel, as you gesture pulling out the dagger or the knife or untwisting the knot.

Step 4: Throw the bad energy away and burn it up with a fire sound like "ssh" so that it disappears.

Step 5: Repeat steps 1-4 until no betraying energy is felt any more in any part of the body.

Step 6: Breathe trust back into your body by giving the feeling of trust a colour and taking three deep breaths. For each breath, breathe in for "1,2,3,4", counts and out for "1,2,3,4,5,6,7,8".

Step 7: Walk around the room saying "I am safe, I am protected" and then create the "d,d,d,d", safety dome around you with your hands.

Further sequences combining attentional deployment and cognitive change.

The following artistic therapy sequences engage both attentional deployment as well as over time cognitive and affective changes. These sequences are designed particularly to deal with the over attachment to low mood and and cognitive and affective focus upon despair that is prevalent in contemporary society particularly among adolescents and "tweens".

Despair to hope (suitable for 11- 16 year olds)
Step 1
Where in your body do you feel the despair? Imagine stepping forward into that part of your body and sense the shape of the stress. Draw the shape using crayon. This is the pre-intervention imprint of despair.

Ask the client to select three people/animals alive or dead, imaginary/real who have experienced difficult circumstances and who should be in despair but have remained hopeful. Commonly used images selected include superheroes, Nelson Mandela, Mother Teresa, a family member, Jesus.

Place around the crayon drawing of the stress of despair the three images of hope selected by the client.

Step 2
Starting with the first person chosen begin a positive resourcing sequence outlined below:

Resourcing sequence
Assess where in the body you feel the stress.
Place your hands on that part of the body.
Visualise the first image that represents the missing quality of hope and imagine receiving this missing quality from your chosen resource.

Emotional Self-Regulation and Artistic Therapies

Breathe in the missing quality of that resource to that part of your body, then let the quality flow throughout your whole body.

Colour your breath the colour of the missing quality of hope and continue to breathe it in for five minutes.

Choose a scarf of that colour and place it around your neck or waist. Stand in the new gesture of the quality of hope that you have just visualised receiving.

Find a sound for the missing quality and make the sound aloud. Use a vowel sound if possible as it increases breathing into the body and helps to relax the physical body. Alternatively, think of a song that inspires you to be hopeful. Play the song or sing it.

Draw a picture in colour representing the new flow of hope just received in the body.

Step 3:

Repeat all of the points in step two again but this time using the second resource image chosen by the client to represent hope.

Step 4:

Repeat all of the points in step two again but this time using the third resource image chosen by the client to represent hope triumphing over despair.

Step 5:

Now ask the client to place the hand on the same part of the body where the initial despair was located. Now sense into that part of the body and draw a single large picture showing the flow of energy in that part of the body having now received hope from these three persons, in the face of the previously despairing experiences. This is the post intervention image that represents the transformation from despair to hope.

Now place the original drawing of the despair on the ground, and the three positive painted images of hope around it. Then place the fifth piece of art, the post intervention: the hopeful one, over the first piece so that the client now has the overall view of cognitive restructuring and emotional deployment that facilitates self-regulation of the trigger situation. This sequence is illustrated in Sherwood (2017, pp.53-59)

Summary

Comparing the pre-intervention and post-intervention images, illustrates how in the post-intervention, the colours lighten, expand, flow, as the breath returns to the part of the body previously contracted by the despairing world view. The dark colours are replaced by bright sunny colours while the flow of the breath is now expressed as clear, free strokes rather than contracted and contorted brush strokes.

These new images also provide the client with positive enhancing visualisations to support them that can be used by the client as a means of attentional deployment. They can then focus attention away from the situation that is triggering. This is a means of cognitive restructuring so that they increase their emotional self-regulation.

Have the client take a photograph on their phone of this final arrangement and if they so desire, they can take the drawings with them to place in a significant place in their home. They can daily renew these images by visualising them and consciously taking a few deep breaths to breathe in these new qualities.

It is recommended they do this for at least seven days.

Betrayal to Trust

Betrayal is a common feeling among broken friendships and in some family situations. Often a client who is cognitively focused upon the betrayal has great difficulty letting go of old situations and experiences and living in the present moment. They lack emotional self-regulation in peer settings particularly in the 11 to 15 year old age group where jealousies and early pairing of genders begins. The betrayal to trust sequence provides the client who has experienced betrayal, to cognitively restructure and engage in attentional deployment towards the positive state of trust.

Initially, clients experience betrayal as a force that has attacked them, and is reflected in the English language as "a knife in the heart", "a knife in the back", or "a kick in the stomach". Clients are asked to visualize, draw, describe, and select an image of how they experience the betrayal in their bodies. If they say a knife in the heart then using gesture and sound, Counsellor and client visualise and gesture pulling out the knife from their heart and throwing it away while breathing out and releasing the contracted breathing. We do this several times then breathe deeply back into the part of the body that experienced the "knife" or whatever force the client describes as having attacked them.

This is followed by the betrayal to trust sequence outlined below using guided imagery and redirecting the client's cognitive and behavioural actions towards emotional self-regulation in face of the trigger situation or person. The betrayal to trust sequence requires the client to choose three images of persons, animals, archetypes or natural images whom they could trust. This sequence follows the same sequential pattern of the preceeding sequence but focuses instead on the movement from betrayal to trust.

Step 1

Ask where in your body do you feel the betrayal? Imagine stepping forward into that part of your body and sense the shape of the stress. Draw the shape with crayons.

Ask them to select three images that the client feels that they could trust. Commonly used persons selected by clients include the Dalai Lama, Nelson Mandela, Mother Teresa, Martin Luther King, Ghandi, Fred Hollows, Christ, Jesus, and Mother Mary, or a family member. Place the crayon drawing of betrayal in the centre and around it the three pictures of the persons whom they can trust.

Step 2
Ask them to start with the first person chosen by the client and begin a positive resourcing sequence which is as follows:
Where in the body do you experience the need for the missing quality of trust.
Place your hands on that place.
Visualise the first image that represents the missing quality of trust and imagine receiving this missing quality from the chosen image.
Breathe into the body the missing quality of trust then let the quality flow throughout your whole body
Colour your breath the colour of the missing quality and continue to breathe it in for 5 minutes.
Stand in the new gesture of the quality of trust that you have just made.
Find a sound for the missing quality of trust and make the sound out loud. Use a vowel sound if possible as it increases breathing into the body and as such helps to relax the physical body. Alternatively think of a song that reminds you of this quality of trust and sing the song or listen to it.
Draw a picture in colour representing the new flow of breath of trust just received that is now flowing through the body. Place this image next to the first image of the betrayed one.

Step 3:
Repeat all of the points in step two again using the second image chosen by the client to represent trust.

Step 4:
Repeat all of the points in step two again but this time using the third image chosen by the client to represent trust.

Step 5:
Now ask the client to place their hands on the same part of the body where the initial feeling of betrayal was located. Now sense into that part of the body and draw a single large picture showing the flow of

energy in that part of the body having now received trust from these three figures.

This is the post intervention image that represents the transformed image that is a result of the cognitive shift from betrayal to trust.

Summary

The pre intervention and post intervention images illustrate how in the post intervention the colours lighten, expand and flow, and all signs of the breath returning to the part of the body previously contracted by the betrayal. The dark imagery of the pre-intervention with its contracted heart is replaced by imagery that has light colours, expansiveness and is flowing and which represents a new gesture for the client's body that is upright and positive. This means more uprightness, more peace and a new positive cognitive perception.

The new images also provide the client with positive enhancing visualisations to support new positive cognitive perceptions of themselves.

Step 6:

Now place the original image on the ground, and the three resources of the images of trust around it. Then place the fifth piece of art, the post intervention: the trusting one, over the first piece so that the client now has the overall view of the guided imagery transformation. The arrangement of all images is the same as in the preceding two sequences.

The client takes a photograph on their phone of this final arrangement and if they so desire, and they may take the drawings with them. They place them in a significant place in their home where they can daily renew these images by visualising them and consciously taking a few deep breaths to breathe in these new qualities.

It is recommended the client complete this exercise every day for at least seven days and in the trigger situation, so that attention is directed towards that trust figures and away from the person/ persons previously experienced as betraying figures.

Conclusion

Attentional deployment can be facilitated by the guided imagery and colour exercises above, so that the client regains emotional self-regulation in triggering situations while also engaging in cognitive restructuring and emotional release.

References

Ferri, J., and Hajcak, G., (2015) Neural mechanisms associated with reappraisal and attentional deployment *CurrOpin Psychol*. 2015 Jun 1; 3: 17–21.doi: 10.1016/j.copsyc.2015.01.010

Bebko, G., Franconeri, S., Oschsner, K., Chiao, J., (2014) *Attentional deployment is not necessary for successful emotion regulation via coitive reappraisal or expressive suppression.* 2014 Jun;14(3):504-512. doi: 10.1037/a0035459. Epub 2014 Feb 10.

Loewenstein, G. (2007). Affect regulation and affective forecasting. In J. J. Gross (Ed.), *Handbook of Emotion Regulation* (pp.180-203). New York: Guilford Press.

Sherwood, P., (2017) *CBT and Artistic Therapies: an unlikely Marriage*, Sophia Publications, Bunbury, Australia.

Van De Kolk, B., (2015) *The Body Keeps the Score*, Penguin, London.

CHAPTER 5

COGNITIVE CHANGE

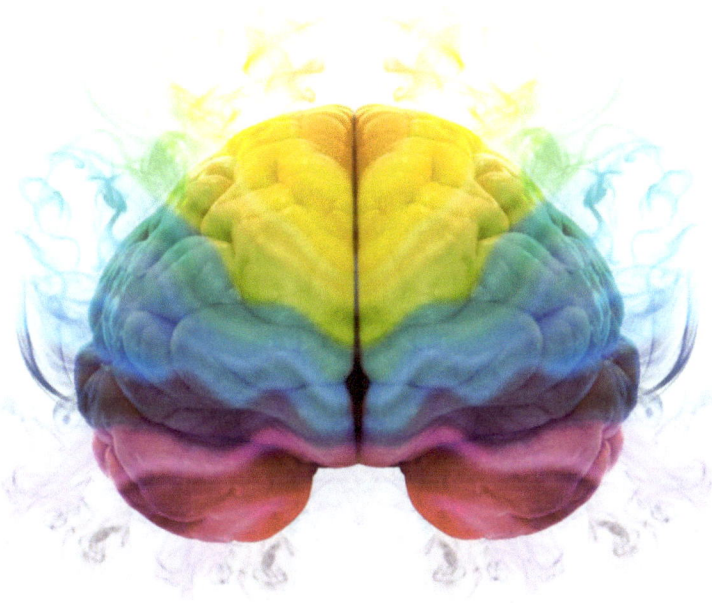

Ref: https://artbusinessnews.com/2015/12/the-expanding-reach-of-art-therapy/

Emotional Self-Regulation and Artistic Therapies

"I create beautiful art, so I can look back on the life my body fell short of in such a way that it brings me peace."
—Nikki Rowe

Introduction

Cognitive change is the most widely used strategy to encourage emotional self-regulation. This involves using a range of cognitive skills including perspective taking, challenging interpretation, reframing, restructuring, visualizing, and avoiding catastrophising by identifying black/white thinking, minimizing and modifying the meaning of a situation or relationship that is triggering emotional dysregulation in the client.

The need to balance the cognitive processes of emotional self-regulation is identified by Kennert et. al. (2016):

> The self-regulation of cognition is the voluntary regulation of thoughts and mental processes to balance between inhibition and initiation of behavior in order to achieve a goal. Mental processes involved may include attention, memory, learning (as well as using prior learning), reasoning, problem-solving, decision-making, metacognition, and motivation around goal directedness. A lack of cognitive self-regulation can result in the individual being unfocused. Too much cognitive regulation can result in obsession.

Lack of cognitive self-regulation will profoundly exacerbate emotional dysregulation in children and adolescents.

In this chapter cognitive reframing will be explored under the following headings:

1. **Reappraisal and reframing**
   This refers to the ability to observe, objectively describe the situation and participate in re-interpreting the situation to self. It can be positive or negative but we will focus on positive reframing and reappraisal as it is the aspect essential to emotional regulation.
2. **Distancing**
   This refers to the capacity to take an independent third person perspective when evaluating an emotional experience so that one's self-reflection may allow for new perspectives to understand and manage the situation. This increases problem solving behaviours and increases the capacity to manage emotions when triggered by the same situation in the future.
3. **Restructuring**
   This refers to the capacity to change one's mind-set from a negative to a positive one by strengthening the self so as to have greater resources to process challenging emotional situations.
4. **Guided image making**
   This refers to imagining an event or series of events with a therapeutic intention. It is promoted by a number of mental health organizations including the adolescent counselling Headspace;

> Guided imagery is a focused practice that involves each of the five senses to ignite positive healing messages throughout the mind and body. The practice is often interchanged with visualisation, self-hypnosis and guided meditation, but it has its own set of techniques. The benefits of guided imagery are vast — there is research that shows the practice can reduce

fear and anxiety, lessen the frequency of headaches and has been proven to decrease psychological distress in cancer patients.
(https://www.headspace.com/meditation/guided-imagery. Accessed 27/2/2023)

Nguyen et al. (2018) demonstrate in their research the capacity of nature based guided imagery to reduce anxiety which is an easily accessible way of accessing positive imagery for children and adolescents.

A meta-review of the research by Pile, et al. cited in the *Lancet Psychiatry*, identifies 86 papers that support positive emotional guided imagery for reducing anxiety and depression. Napastek, (2022) reviews the research findings:

> By that they mean imagery designed to generate positive feelings, (think contentment, gratitude, inspiration, confidence, love, optimism, trust…} or, alternatively, imagery designed to subvert or redirect negative feelings (think fear, shame, anger, resentment, bitterness, self-criticism, hopelessness, self-doubt…) The authors identified three imagery techniques that emerged as particularly efficacious. They were:

- imagery techniques that guided the listener to relive fantasies places, people or experiences that generated positive feelings,
- imagery rescripting therapy – rewriting history in the imagination with a remediating, positive slant, to overtake and supplant the painful charge of a traumatic or disturbing memory,

- imagery-enhanced protocols, such as Eye Movement Desensitisation and Reprocessing therapy (EMDR), Prolonged Exposure, Imagery Rehearsal Therapy, and the like.

Addressing the obstacles to cognitive reappraisal in traumatized clients

Cognitive reappraisal and emotional self-regulation depend upon being in touch with the body because our sensory interiority continually sends us message about the needs of our organism such as whether we are hungry, tired but additionally whether we feel safe with a person, unsafe, or threatened and our language reflects this. I have a "gut feeling" that this is not great. They make my "skin crawl". I feel that person is "slimy and slippery" or I feel "the sleaze after that person looks at me and I want to have shower". We regularly are reading our bodies interior messages in response to the external environment, people around us, as well as our own internal environment. Sensing and breathing are our very first languages and they are designed to keep us safe. However, traumatised persons have experienced such sensory trauma through fear, violence, threats, rapes or the like that they have survived by cutting off their awareness of their bodily messages. Van De Kolk (2015,p. 93) notes that Magnetic Resonance Imaging (MRI) scans of chronic PTSD patients show almost no activation of any of the self sensing areas of the brain. He goes on to describe this process:

> ...traumatized people chronically feel unsafe inside their bodies. The past is alive in the form of gnawing interior discomfort. Their bodies are constantly bombarded by visceral warning signs and in an attempt

> control these processes, they often become expert at ignoring their gut feelings and in numbing awareness of what is played out inside, the more people try to push away and ignore internal warning signs, the more likely they are to take over and leave them bewildered, confused and ashamed...they become vulnerable to respond to any sensory shift either by shutting down or going into a panic.. they develop a fear of fear itself (Van De Kolk 2015, p.99).

They are highly prone to emotional dysregulation and/or grasp at drugs, prescribed or otherwise, or other addictive habits to try to manage the distress and discomfort which they have no full consciousness of and which they cannot name. This phenomenon is called alexithymia or not having words for feelings. They can name behaviours but their feelings are blunted.

> ...traumatized people often have trouble sensing what is going on in their bodies, they lack a nuanced response to frustration. They either react to stress by becoming spaced out or with excessive anger. Whatever their response, they often can't tell what is upsetting them. This failure to be in touch with their bodies contributes to their well-documented lack of self-protection and high rates of revictimization and also to their remarkable difficulties feeling pleasure, sensuality and having a sense of meaning (Van De Kolk, 2015, p.101).

Dr. Patricia Sherwood

Traumatised children and adolescents, those least able to emotionally self-regulate will not successfully apply cognitive reappraisal strategies unless they first find a language for their feelings. To know their feelings, they must become familiar with the sensations of their bodies. The first step is to redevelop their sensing. Gendlin (1967) developed a technique called "focusing" to facilitate this awareness in clients:

> What is focusing? Based on research at the University of Chicago, focusing is a new technique of self therapy that teaches you to identify and change the way your personal problems concretely exist in your body. Focusing consists of steps of felt change. Unlike methods that stress "getting in touch with your feelings," there is a built-in test- each focusing step, when done correctly, is marked by a physical relief, a profound release of tension. Focusing guides you to the deepest level of awareness within your body. It is on this level, unfamiliar to most people, that unresolved problems actually exist, and only on this level can they change.(https://www.amazon.com.au/Focusing-Eugene-T-Gendlin/dp/0553278339. Accessed 28/2/2023.)

Essentially, focusing with its six steps is a process for deeply sensing into the parts of your body where the stress or tension is held in a particular situation, to come to an awareness of the underlying emotion and possibly, also the initial trauma in some cases. This bringing to consciousness of core traumatic experiences, naming them and recognising them involves releasing the breathing that is contracted in that part of the body. Once the breath is released the client is more able to become present to the present moment and to understand the nature of their feelings in a particular situation.

Van De Kolk (2015,pp102-3) describes this process as "befriending the body", essential for emotional self-regulation. He notes:

> Angry people live in angry bodies. The bodies of child abuse victims are tense and defensive until they find a way to relax and feel safe. In order to change, people need to become aware of their sensations and the way that their bodies interact with the world around them. Physical self awareness is the first step to releasing the tyranny of the past.

With practice and redeveloping the sensing capacity of the physical body, clients who lack emotional awareness and an emotional vocabulary are able over time to connect physical sensations to underlying feelings and psychological events and experiences in their lives. They are able to rediscover the ability to be aware of the joys, frustrations and sorrows of human existence and to begin to learn to manage these feelings.

The artistic based therapies that are documented in this book aim to do precisely this. These sequences always engage sensing into the body as the preliminary step to become aware of where tension is held in the body and the breathing contracted. The purpose of the interventions is to release the breath at these sites and in so doing open the door of the unconscious for the emotions to surface, be named and identified and then to be processed. At this stage in the therapy, one is able to build upon the techniques of cognitive reappraisal to strengthen the clients newly developed sense of feeling and to assist in the identification of self-regulation strategies. The theoretical details of this process, the model and associated techniques for intervention particularly for children and adolescents are documented in Sherwood (2013,2009,2008, 2007).

1. The Artistic therapies and Cognitive reappraisal.

The artistic therapies are excellent in reconnecting the unconscious trauma that is frozen deep within the psyche and which is experienced by contracted breathing. These patterns result in stress stored within different parts of the body and which in the long term oftimes result in illness. Through gesture, movement, and the nonverbal languages of sensing, visualising and breathing, clients are reconnected to the blocked emotions. Through these sequences they are given artistic activities to release the trauma and restore the breathing and self-awareness or "presence' to that part of the body.

Many of these exercises engage cognitive reappraisal/reframing, restructuring, distancing and guided imagery concurrently, but they will be elucidated under the four headings based upon their primary intent.

Compassion triangle: for dealing with guilt and judgment by others.

Guilt has claws which keep the client living in the past while the beauty and joy of the present moment remains unseen and unacknowledged. The client is in the clutches of other's judgments which have become an internalised voice that condemns them for not living up to certain standards, for failing to behave in an acceptable way.

The compassion triangle, developed by Tagar (1996), is a profoundly revelatory process for separating out the critic or judge from the compassionate or non judgmental one within each of us and in the process reframing the client's experience of failure into an experience of self acceptance and healthy growth. It liberates the client from the prison of self-judgment and self rejection and frees them to be available to self acceptance of themselves and of others despite their human limitations. This sequence demonstrates how reframing, by enlarging the power of compassion through changing the thought patterns that maintain self condemnation and guilt, into self acceptance and loving kindness, liberate the client to live life more fully.

The three positions in the compassion triangle.

The points of the triangle represent the 3 primary psychotherapeutic positions within each human psyche. They are placed and so named on the ground ready for the client to use in the process.

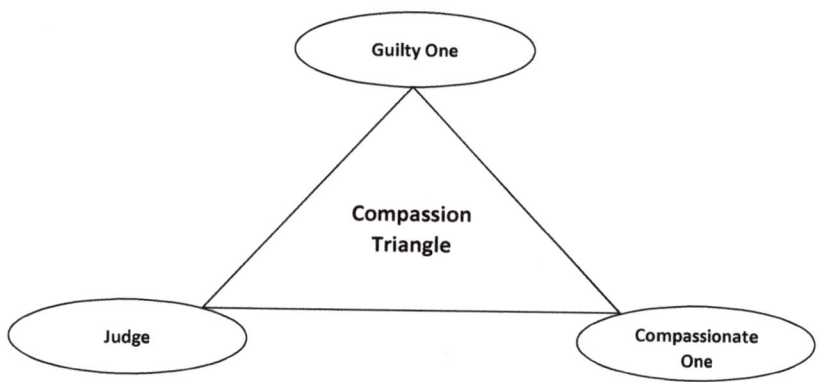

1. **The guilty one**

    The first position is the part of the psyche that is wounded, that carries the imprint of pain and trauma in relation to the experience of guilt and failure.

2. **The judge**

    The second position in the compassion triangle is the part which reacts to the condemned one with judgment and blame and creates the psychic position of judgment or the judge. The judge is always a voice of a significant other, a parent, sibling, teacher or other power holder in the client's world, present or past or both, that provides the initial imprint for condemnation and judgment. Eventually, after repeated assaults, the child comes to internalise the judge voice that "I am to blame" and continues as an adult, to run this message. The extent of the judgment is measured by the number of judges, their psychic height and the intensity of condemnation in the tone of the client when speaking through the psychic part of the judge.

3. **The compassionate one**

    The third position is the part which is capable of compassion, kindness and of understanding. It is the reservoir of the positive self healing qualities. This is the position of unconditional positive regard. It is the place of unlimited nourishing and healing resources that is either already developing within the client but needs to be enlarged, or which can be created by the client through accessing archetypal images of compassion and forgiveness.

Sequential processes in the compassion triangle

The process of this sequence has been adapted by Sherwood from Tagar's original notion (1996) and is described below: To begin a compassion triangle the client needs to recall a specific instance with a specific person in which they felt guilty or a failure and to sense where the disturbance is experienced in their body.

Stage 1. "Enter-exit-behold": visualizing how the judgment in the body is experienced.

The client senses where they feel the tension in the body and take a step forward visualizing stepping into that part of the body. They are asked to sense the shape of the tension stored there, which is the contracted breathing and then to step backwards and draw the shape of the contracted breathing with crayons on paper. Then the client is asked to step forwards again and insert their whole body in into the shape they have drawn. While the client is in the contracted gesture, they are asked to identify the earliest memory of their body being in that shape. Usually, the client recalls a childhood incident in which they are being judged, which has vibrational resonance with the presenting issues of judgment as an adolescent of adult. This position of trauma of the condemned one is marked on the ground with a cushion. This enables the client to view the trauma from an emotional distance by stepping backwards and away from the cushion, if the experience of the trauma is overwhelming. It creates distancing which facilitates insight and reduces the potential for flooding or trauma re-enactment.

Stage 2. "Enter-exit-behold": developing insight into the judge position

The Counsellor asks the client to enter into or step forward into the position marked on the ground of the voice of condemnation and judgment and while in this position to sense the fury, anger, judgment and condemnation that the client feels about the judged one. Ask the client to speak out these feelings out loud to the condemned one, so they can hear the harshness and sense the ugliness of the judgment gesture.

Ask the client to turn around and look behind their back and to tell you who they see standing there joining in the chorus of condemnation. There will usually be a group of key judges in their life: such as a parent, sibling, and teacher.

Ask the client how tall are the judges. The number of judges and their height indicates the extent of the self condemnation and guilt. A large number of tall judges will usually suggest that a number of compassion triangles will be needed, at least one for each of the significant judge voices as a general rule.

Ask the client to gesture and draw this judge voice until its qualities of ugliness and aversive control are very clear.

Stage 3. "Enter-exit-behold": understanding the compassionate voice

The client enters into the position of the compassionate voice which can be marked by a cushion representing an apex of the triangle. Here the client is asked to observe the judged one from the position of understanding and loving kindness.

Ask the client to speak from the voice of understanding, which is the voice of compassion that embraces human limitations, weaknesses, exhaustion and overwhelm. Sometimes the client cannot access this voice within themselves because it has been so extinguished in their life. Then it is essential to stop the process and go and find a compassionate figure in their life. One needs only to find one voice, a teacher, a friend, a significant adult who understood and valued the client. If one cannot be found then the client needs to go to the resourcing position and access an archetypal resource such as the Kwan Yin, Cannon, Krishna, Jesus or Mary from whom they can receive compassion and who can speak through the client to the inner part of them self with compassion. When the client has completed speaking to the judged one from the compassionate position, the Counsellor asks the client to turn around and look at who stands behind them. The height and the number of persons standing here indicate the client's compassionate resources. This process inevitably takes the client to the position of compassion towards self and creates a space for the expression of deep feelings, particularly grief. The client gestures and draws the feelings of this position of beauty, softness of heart and the loving embrace of compassion.

Stage 4. The empowerment sequence: removing the imprint of the judge

The next task is to release the contracted breathing resulting from the judges' voices. The client enters back into the contracted gesture of the condemned one, to find how the voice/condemnation of the judge which the client experiences as "the force," which contracts their breathing. Do they feel attacked by a knife, arrows, a punch, a kick, a dagger? Does the force of judgment feel to be a one off or repetitive?

Once the client has identified their felt experience of the force of judgement have them show you the force on a cushion so that they can see the sound and gesture of this force that is contracting their breathing and causing stress in their lives. Then have the client reverse the force. For example, if they experience a dagger as "nnnn": and they reverse it by saying out loud "nah" and literally using gesture to pull it out and throw it away ending with a vowel such as "ahh".

All contracted breathing and stresses are stored in the consonant sounds and all stress is released by opening of the breath through in vowels sounds. Ask the client to draw the flow of compassionate energy now moving through their body, that they received from the person they used as a compassion archetype.

Stage 5. Resourcing and invoking: accessing the powerful compassionate resources

This is followed by returning to the place on the ground that represents the compassion voice and enlarging that voice using a resourcing sequence outlined on pages 86-87, but using a compassionate figure as the source of the resourcing need for understanding and self acceptance.

Stage 6. Consolidating the reframing

Ask the client to now step into the position of the judge voice marked by the cushion on the ground and turn around and tell you how tall they now experience the judge voices. Ask them to do so also with the compassion voices. If the reframing has been successful, the height of the judges will have reduced at the end of the session and the height of the compassionate ones will have increased. In addition, the client will now have reframed judgment experiences to become aware that they have a choice as to which voice they accept: their voice of judgment or the voice of compassion when they are in similar circumstances.

Chair dialogue

This is a dramatherapy technique that facilitates reframing and re-appraisal for the client and which is very powerful in assisting with emotional self regulation. This technique is elucidated by Pugh (2017):

> Three core forms of chair work have been described within the literature (Kellogg, 2015; Pugh, 2017). In empty-chair exercises, the individual is encouraged to engage in a dialogue with an imagined other placed in an empty seat. This 'other' may be an actual individual (as demonstrated in Susan's confrontation with her mother) or something symbolic (for example, a personal goal or one's 'inner critic'). In two-chair exercises, the individual is asked to move between chairs representing different perspectives or parts of the self. For example, two chairs may be used to

represent the part of the self that wants to change a behaviour and the part that does not, or one's 'rational' versus 'emotional' side. Finally, the therapist and the client may (re-)enact problematic interactions through the medium of chair work ('chair work role-plays'). This may be with a view to better understand events from the past, reality-test interactions in the present, rehearse behaviours for the future, or simply aid perspective taking.

This technique was developed by Moreno initially for psychodrama but has been applied in one to one client encounters most effectively by Perls, and the Gestalt therapists. It is a powerful technique for facilitating development of empathy, the creation of choices, and developing new perspectives on any problem situation as well as understanding of different viewpoints. It is particularly helpful for work with adolescents who tend to enjoy dramatherapy approaches to reappraising their presenting issues.

Distancing
Distancing is an excellent strategy for reviewing a situation from a more objective and emotionally regulated position and dramatherapy actually provides a number of bodily experiences that assist with this process.

Boundaries
Maintaining boundaries and the "safety dome" is a dramatherapy technique outlined in pages 25 which involves building a safety dome using the blocking sound"d,d,d,d". When clients practice this daily for

1 minute, they discover that they are more able to develop a strategic depth of perspective on a given situation.

Exiting

This is another dramatherapy technique; developed by Tagar (1996) involving bodily gesture and sound which are most effective in assisting a client obtain a strategic distance on a triggering situation, whether fear or anger. It works very well if the client repeats it daily to clear any emotionally accumulated feelings as well being applied aat the moment of being triggered. This is documented on pages 29-30.

Staging

This technique developed by Tagar, can be used to distance oneself from a trigger or trauma situation. The person first exits once, then places a cushion on the ground to indicate the original position of emotional dysregulation. Instead of the cushion, a doll can be used or soft toy. Then walking around in a circle, they view and remark on the what they see from different angles in the room as they look back at the triggering situation represented by the cushion/doll/soft toy. The client will begin to discover amazing new insights about the trigger situation of which they were previously unaware. This is a very effective dramatherapy distancing and staging technique and suitable for a wide variety of ages.

Family of Origin in clay

This sequence enables the client to reframe and re-appraise their family of origin as experiences in their family system becomes visible. It enables the client to start to create insights into how these are affecting their presenting issue. It is completed in clay and externalises the feelings that a client has in relation to different family members. This technique was developed by Sherwood (2004).

Step 1:
- Ask the client to make the number of hand sized round balls of clay for the number of influential family members, that is significant family members who were/are present in their family of origin. Add an extra ball to represent the client.

Step 2
- Request that the client thinks of their father and an experience that was typical or is typical of their relationship. This father may be biological or adoptive. If more than one father, then the client completes a piece for each one.
- Client recalls in detail the experience, the physical surroundings and any other physical details.
- Client finds where in their body they feel the strongest sensation as they recall the experience.
- They gesture the feeling in this place in their body with both hands. Does it feel like a knot, a lump, a hollow or some other shape?
- Client takes a piece of clay and shapes it into a form that represents the gesture of the experience of the father that they have sensed.
- When completed the client looks back on the clay piece and notes down the feelings that arise as they behold this piece.

Step 3
Repeat this above sequence with each of the significant members of the family, one at a time until there is a clay model of experience for each family member. Then ask the client to gesture how they feel when they look at these family members and to make in the last ball of clay the shape of the feelings that they experience.

Step 4
On completion of all of the models of the client's family members, ask the client to arrange the pieces in relationship to each other as they express their experience of living in the family system. This then provides a depiction of the family system that gives both the counsellor and the client the opportunity to gain new insights and awareness about their family system. Here is the opportunity to reframe and reappraise particular experiences in their life as they place them into the wider context of their family. In doing this, it empowers the client to understand how they might work to change unhealthy dynamics and enlarge the healthy dynamics.

In clay, emotion is expressed in gesture and it is always important to review the gestures with the client. Are the shapes flowing and upright representing a bodily experience of relaxation and ease or are the pieces contracted, hollowed out, crushed, and confined representing the bodily experience of contracted breathing and bodily stress?

Empathy creation for distancing while engaging those in conflict.
Emotional self-regulation is also promoted by this exercise in clay therapy which assists the client to understand the other person's experience. It is also a distancing technique.

Instructions
Ask two persons in conflict or with unresolved communication issues to sit face to face. One is chosen to begin and takes the role of story teller first, and the other takes the role of listener. The listener is the one who is demonstrating through this exercise their capacity for empathy. The story teller shares their experience with the other

person in five minutes. They will be required to repeat it with accuracy, three times. The listener then responds to the story as detailed below.

Step 1: sculpture in clay the shape representing the listener's response to the story.
- Story teller recounts the incident for five minutes.
- Listening partner senses into his/her own feelings about the incident.
- Listening partner upon completion of the incident selects ball of clay and makes their own feeling response to the story in clay

Step 2: sculpture in clay the shape representing the feelings of the person telling the story.
- Story teller again recounts the incident and their feelings for the second time for five minutes
- Listening partner senses into the story teller's feeling of the story.
- Listening partner upon completion of the story selects a ball of clay and makes the story teller's feeling in clay (this reflects the capacity for empathy).

Step 3: to reflect on the responses.
- Person who has made the two clay pieces reflects on the differences in shape of their feelings versus the story tellers' feelings and is encouraged to understand the story tellers' feelings
- They then explain to the story teller why they made that shape and what they think the story tellers' feelings are about the experience.
- Story teller then responds to the shape representing their feelings and how accurate or otherwise they felt it to be.

Now proceed to repeat the above exercises but on this occasion, the roles are reversed. The listener becomes the storyteller who is telling their story about their feelings in relation to the said incident and the person who was previously the storyteller now becomes the listener who must make the response in clay.

Clay provides a medium for the client to externalize feelings in a concrete form. It makes the invisible visible, the intangible tangible, and in so doing facilities distancing from the experience of conflict or emotional dysregulation, while also providing a window into the feelings of the persons in conflict that is touchable and knowable.

Masks: identifying the two sides of a potential response in a trigger situation

Children and particularly adolescents enjoy the use of masks as a method for distancing themselves from a situation while also exploring possible responses. Children tend to choose animal masks while adolescents prefer carnival type or archetypal masks of evil or positive images.

Step 1:
- Client chooses two masks that represent the positive and negative potential responses to the trigger incident.
- These masks are best if created by the client although some archetypal masks may be chosen if available.

Step 2:
- Client speaks through the negative masks enlarging the situation in which the response represents emotional dysregulation
- Client then exits and debriefs about that mask experience.

Step 3:
- The client then chooses the mask that is positive and represents emotional regulation.
- The client speaks from this mask position.

- Client then compares the two voices and reflects with the therapist on which would be the most skilful mask to wear in the trigger situation.

Masks are an ideal drama therapy technique to develop a sense of distancing and therefore increase the capacity of the client for cognitive reappraisal and reframing.

Sandplay

This is an ideal artistic therapy that promotes distancing from a trigger situation while simultaneously facilitating deeper emotional experience arising from the subconscious. This experience can be expressed, identified and transformed through experiencing the use of images to represent the experience. The possibilities for sandplay as a method for cognitive change and emotional regulation are profound. Two books recommended to understand and explore further this process are Pearson (2000) and Sherwood (2018). The former gives an excellent introduction to sandplay that is unstructured. The latter specializes in sandplay for trauma recovery and cognitive change.

3. Restructuring

Self condemnation to self forgiveness sequence

In this process of cognitive change, the self of the client is strengthened so they are more able to maintain an emotionally regulated state of being in relation to themselves, others and the world. This is an excellent sequence using guided imagery to facilitate clients moving from self condemnation to self forgiveness. Self condemnation can be a major psychological obstacle for a client keeping them in a cycle of self rejection and making them vulnerable to emotional trigger situations, which they can perceive as judgment and react with emotional outbursts because they experience it as an attack upon their self esteem and competency. If they can shore up their own sense of self worth, then the likelihood of such a trigger response is reduced significantly. In addition, self condemnation and the associated shame often encourage behaviours that make emotional regulation even more challenging. These include self sabotaging behaviours such as addictions. Through negative thinking, the client holds tenaciously to an image of themselves as faulty, inadequate and in some ways hopeless, helpless or useless. This exercise provides alternative imagery suggestions and supports the development of a positive internal dialogue.

This guided imagery sequence provides alternative positive self forgiving and self accepting imagery for the client that if repeated daily for at least seven days, can facilitate the client making transformative changes towards more skilful cognitions and behaviours towards themselves and others. The self forgiveness sequence requires the client to choose images of three figures who could forgive them when they find they cannot forgive themselves. This exercise can be completed in watercolour, oil crayons or acrylic paint.

Step 1
- Ask the client where in your body do you feel the self condemnation? Imagine stepping forward into that part of your body and sense the shape of the breath. Draw the shape in crayon. This is the pre intervention imprint of self condemnation.
- Suggest that the client select and name three images of people or animals who could forgive them. Commonly used persons selected by clients include the Dalai Lama, Nelson Mandela, Mother Teresa, Martin Luther King, Gandhi, Fred Hollows, Thich Nat Hahn, Sister Chan Khong. Other images often chosen include one's dog, auntie, grandmother or some other forgiving person they have known personally in their life.

Emotional Self-Regulation and Artistic Therapies

- Place the self condemnation image in the centre and around that image, the three pictures of the persons or animals that have been chosen who could forgive them.

Step 2
- Starting with the first person chosen by the client begin a positive resourcing sequence which is as follows:
- Where in the body do your experience the need for the missing quality of self forgiveness.
- Place your hands on that part of your body.
- Visualize the first image that represents the missing quality of self forgiveness and imagine receiving this missing quality from them.
- Breathe in the missing quality to that part of your body, and then let the quality flow throughout your whole body.
- Colour your breath the colour of the missing quality and continue to breathe it in for five minutes
- Stand in the new gesture of the quality of self forgiveness that you have just visualized receiving (in this example the client chose their dog).
- Find a sound for the missing quality and make the sound aloud. Use a vowel sound if possible as it increases breathing into the body and as such helps to relax the physical body. Alternatively think of a song that reminds you of this quality of self forgiveness
- Draw a picture in colour representing the new flow of breath of self forgiveness just received in the body. Place this image next to the image from which they have chosen to resource

Step 3:
- Repeat all of the points in step two again but this time using the second image chosen by the client to represent self forgiveness. Place this next to image two of self-forgiveness that the client has selected.

Step 4:
- Repeat all of the points in step two again but this time using the third image chosen by the client to represent self forgiveness. Place this picture next to the third image of self forgiveness that the client has selected.

Step 5:
- Now ask the client to place their hands on the same part of the body where the initial self condemnation was located. Now sense into that part of the body and draw a single large picture showing the flow of energy in that part of the body having now received self forgiveness from these three persons/animals. This is the post intervention image that represents the transformation from self condemnation to self forgiveness. Place this on top of the image of self condemnation (the unforgivable one). Photograph the complete set of images of self forgiveness especially the final painting which is cumulative of all of the self forgiveness energies.

Summary

The pre intervention and post intervention images illustrate how in the post intervention the colours lighten, expand and flow, all signs of the breath returning to the part of the body previously contracted by the self condemnation. The new images also provide the client with positive enhancing visualizations to support new positive cognitive perceptions of themselves which provide foundational images for positive internal dialogue, cognitive and behavioural changes. When repeated daily they strengthen the self of the client and in so doing strengthen their capacity for maintaining emotional regulation.

Shame (low self-esteem) to self-esteem art therapy exercise.

Low self esteem children and adults who are underachievers, often hold deeply sabotaging beliefs about themselves, and are highly prone to irrational, negative cognitive patterns. Shame is deeply rooted at the core of the individual's self esteem. It is comprised of messages from others that devalue the child in such profound ways that these toxic statements undermine the individual's capacity to self-regulate as they are prone to relate to the conversations and situations around them as negative. Because they perceive themselves negatively: "I am worthless", "I am stupid", "I am hopeless", "I am incompetent", "I am useless", "I am lazy", and "I am unlovable", they are likely to hear these negative messages in conversations with others even when they were not intended. Central to low self esteem are major cognitive distortions including polarised thinking, overgeneralising, disqualifying the positive, magnification, emotional reasoning, jumping to conclusions, catastrophising and personalisation. These cause the individual to perceive reality in ways that undermine their capacity for emotional regulation and which in the long term can produce anxiety, depression, despair and addictive behaviours.

The low self-esteem "shame" tree: a profile of negative internal dialogue.

The client who wishes to improve their self-esteem begins by filling in a low self esteem or shame tree, each root representing one of the core toxic cognitive messages of failure or devaluation that the client believes.

A self esteem tree is then filled in which contains the same number of roots as the toxic tree but with each root representing the positive alternative messages that are a result of the cognitive restructuring. These trees become the diagnostic counselling plan for the number of counselling sessions and types of interventions required. Common core messages in the self-esteem tree that have been sabotaged by negative cognitive worldviews are:

I am intelligent.
I am hard working.
I am worthwhile.
I am attractive.
I am knowledgeable.
I am competent.
I am lovable.
I am useful.

Each of the core messages in the high self esteem tree becomes the cognitive restructuring goal for the therapy session. So, for example, the "I am stupid" low self-esteem message is exposed as all or nothing thinking, overgeneralising, magnification and personalisation to the client and the alternative message, the new positive esteem building message, in this case, "I am intelligent" replaces it. The concretisation of this positive world view occurs post session through exercises that affirm this reality. A therapy session is devoted to each low self esteem message initially identified in session one, until all the cognitive thinking distortions that underlie the low self esteem tree have been explored and replaced with positive rational, cognitive messages that support the restructuring of the clients self and strengthen it.

Sand tray exercise for Body Dysmorphia Disorder

Sandplay is a particularly powerful art therapy for restructuring and strengthening the self whether structured or unstructured, directed or nondirected. The example below is a structured sandplay intervention working with body dysmorphia which is defined as follows:

BDD is a body-image disorder characterized by persistent and intrusive preoccupations with an imagined or slight defect in one's appearance. People with BDD can dislike any part of their body, although they often find fault with their hair, skin, nose, chest, or stomach. In reality, a perceived defect may be only a slight imperfection or nonexistent. But for someone with BDD, the flaw is significant and prominent, often causing severe emotional distress and difficulties in daily functioning. (https://adaa.org/understanding-anxiety/body-dysmorphic-disorder, Accessed 6-3-2023.)

Sandplay sequences
Prior to commencing these directed sandplay sequences, the Therapist will invite the client to complete some nondirective sandplay, so that the client familiarises themselves with the technique of sandplay. This is a summary, a cameo (small part of the client's life) of what can be achieved with sandplay. A full therapeutic application of this sequence is elucidated in Sherwood (2018, pp55-72).

1. Sandplay sequence showing the battle for the body between the self and the anti-self

Step 1:
- Ask the client to choose a piece that represents the critical voice that is continually belittling and criticising their body. The size of the piece chosen reflects the level of power that the client experiences that this voice has over their life.
- Invite the client to select a piece that represents their self, the best of who they can be. The size of this piece represents the power they experience in relation to their positive self.

Step 2:
- Suggest the client select a figurine that represents their body and place it between the critical voice which we call the anti-self and the piece that represents their self.

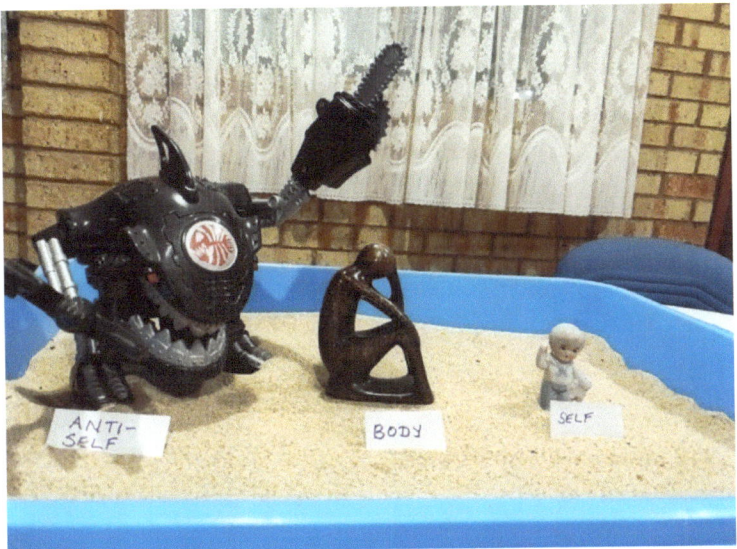

The anti-self versus the self for control of their body

Reflection
Identify that this is a battle for their body between their self, and the anti-self. The battle between the anti-self and the self for the client's body is established and the goal of therapy is to disempower the anti-self because it is costing the client friends, work, health and happiness, and to re-empower the self.

Sandplay sequence to understand the weapons of the anti-self used in the battle against the self to win possession of the client's body

Step 1:
- Ask the client to place in the sandtray figurines representing the anti-self or critical voice and their body.

- Invite the client to choose a figurine that represents their self, the one that is afflicted by the negative critical voices of the anti-self that is constantly belittling and shaming their body or parts thereof.

Step 2:
- Invite the client to write down all the negative feelings that the anti-self directs towards the self. In this example there are three of these negative feelings representative of the types of negative feelings that clients' express: namely self-loathing, self-annihilation and self criticism.
- Suggest the client find figurines that represent each of these attacks upon the self by the anti-self and have them place these pieces in the tray in relation to the self.

The weapons of the anti-self against the self.

Reflections

Ask the client to identify clearly why the self is losing the battle and why the anti-self is winning. Request the client to write down the negative messages that the self has internalised as a result of being defeated in this battle with the anti-self.

2. Sandplay sequence to empower the self and place boundaries against the anti-self controlling their body and their life.

Step 1:
- Invite the client to select figurines that represent their self and their body and place them in the sandtray.
- Invite the client to list all the positive messages that are now part of the cognitive framework of the self, having completed the somatic sequences above namely: "I am attractive, I am a success, I am lovable" and "I am useful" as in this example.
- Select figurines that represent these positive messages and place then around the self.

Step 2:
- Now select a figurine to represent the anti-self and place in the sandtray with a significant boundary around it.

Emotional Self-Regulation and Artistic Therapies

The self winning the battle for the body by overcoming the anti-self.

Reflection

Invite the client to make a daily practice of placing a boundary between their body and the anti-self.

3. Sandplay sequence of the empowered self winning the battle for the body

Step 1:
- Ask the client to place figurines of themself, and their body in the sandtray.
- Invite the client to choose figurines that represent the new cognitive affective messages that the empowered self is now capable of manifesting, which include in this example: "I am lovable, I am useful, I am attractive" and "I am a success."

Step 2:
- Ask the client to select a figurine that now represents the anti-self and place in the sand tray
- Invite the client to re-arrange the sandtray or remove or add pieces as they now observe and experience the dynamic between the body, the self and the anti-self.

The empowered self winning the battle for the body

Reflection

By this stage in the sandplay work which has occurred over several weeks, the anti-self has considerably diminished in size or is no longer represented. The piece representing the self has enlarged considerably and the piece representing the body is now usually upright and strong and has a powerful rather than oppressed position in the sandtray.

In summary, there are several art therapy exercises, of which I have just identified a few, to assist in revealing cognitive distortions to clients in a very concrete observable manner and which can support clients to move forward, and restructure their experiences in a cognitively rational manner that strengthens their positive self.

4. Guided imagery

The artistic therapies are particularly powerful means for facilitating guided imagery because of the fluency of sensory languages of colour, sound, gesture, visualizing and sensing. Guided imagery is a very powerful technique for introducing cognitive change as documented by Sherwood (2018). Three examples are presented below.

1. Grief and loss recovery sequence

The objective is to restore relaxed and deep breathing in the client's body because breathing becomes shallow and contracted during grief and loss experiences. This sequence incorporates guided imagery that provides positive images upon which the client can rebuild positive, functional behaviours and perceptions to move forward in their life. This process also provides a visual process for the client to track changes in their emotions and cognitions around their grief and loss.

This exercise can be completed in watercolour, acrylics, oil pastels or in clay. Indigenous clients generally prefer clay as do many males. Watercolour is more suitable for the aged, children, convalescing persons, clients who are not robust physically, are exhausted, have chronic fatigue, or express a preference to work in watercolour rather than clay or acrylic paints.

Step 1:
- Ask the client to locate in their body where they feel the sadness
- Suggest that they sense into the felt stress and the associated colours and shapes in that part of their body and paint the colours.

- Avoid painting of visual pictures, rather encourage the client to paint the shape of the place in their body where the feel the stress or emptiness.

Step 2:
- Request the client to name the quality they have lost when they think of their sadness. Is it joy, friendship, warmth, love, fun, companionship.
- Ask them to select an image of someone spiritual or human, living or dead, animal or image from nature that represents the missing quality and imagine breathing in this missing quality from them.
- Suggest that they now breathe in the missing quality to that part of their body, and then let the quality flow throughout their whole body.
- Instruct them to reflect on the colour of the missing quality as it flows through their body. Draw a picture in colour representing the new flow of breath in the body

Step 3:
- Now ask them to sense how the missing quality is flowing through their breathing.
- Request that they now paint how the initial place in which they experienced the sadness is starting to change. (This sequence is illustrated in Sherwood (2017, pp45-7)

At the completion of this exercise, it is helpful to discuss with the client strategies for bringing more of the missing quality back into their life. This includes exploring different dimensions of the client's life including social, personal, work and family contexts if relevant.

Encourage them to implement one of the strategies before the next session and to complete it in a routine regular pattern. An example is joining a social group of their interest that meets weekly or fortnightly, to deal with their loss of friendship or connectedness. This exercise focuses on changing cognitive perceptions and consequently behaviour through a change in their lifestyle.

The client leaves the session with clear instructions in writing of how to repeat the guided imagery sequence that they have just completed in the therapy session. Each day they may choose a different missing quality if that is what is uppermost in their thoughts on that day. They can choose the same quality for several days in a row, if this is dominant in their thinking at the time. Ask the client to date each set of three paintings (that is paintings 1, 2, and 3) and place them consecutively in a plastic leafed folder or something similar. It is desirable that they repeat this process for at least seven days but up to 21 days is better. An example of this guided visualisation exercise is illustrated in Sherwood (2008, p.69).

Mandala sequence for building self-esteem.
Jung was the first psychotherapist to popularize the therapeutic benefits of mandalas. They are currently a popular tool among some art therapists;

> Research studies conducted in the area of psychology have used mandalas as a component to see if the use of mandalas can help reduce stress. Mandalas are also used in art therapy. The Therapist uses a mandala created by the client as a representation of his or her current feelings and emotions. This technique is found to be self-calming and self-centring by some. (Prayoshara 2020).

Dr. Patricia Sherwood

Reducing negative mood through mandala creation by Babouchkina and Robbins (2015) demonstrates an interesting comparison between colouring a square versus a circle that indicates the power of the circle form to induce calm and positivity into a person's mood:

> This study examined whether the creation of a mandala has specific efficacy for reducing negative mood states. A convenience sample of 67 adult participants was randomly assigned to one of 4 conditions following negative mood induction: (a) coloring a blank circle with instructions to express feelings, (b) coloring a blank circle with instructions to draw freely, (c) coloring a square with instructions to express feelings, or (d) coloring a square with instructions to draw freely. The two circle (mandala) groups reported significantly greater mood improvement compared to the two square conditions. These results demonstrate that the circular shape of the mandala serves as an "active ingredient" in mood enhancement.

The circle form is symbolic and also used by some therapists to strengthen and integrate the self. In this exercise, the client is encouraged to identify positive images that strengthen their resources so as to better manage emotional challenges and potential emotional dysregulation.

Mandala for strengthening client's resources to manage emotional dysregulation
Step 1: Draw circle and within it draw three circles.

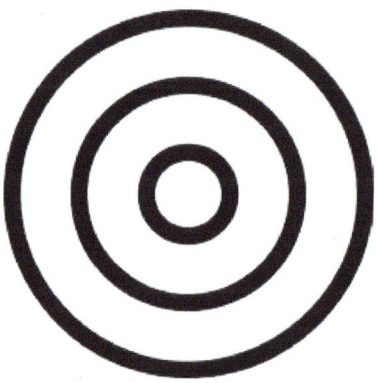

Step 2: Select three symbols: your core symbol, a nurturing symbol, and a protective symbol

Step 3: The core symbol is drawn in the centre of the Mandala.

Step 4: A nurturing symbol is drawn in a repeated pattern in the second symbol that is a symbol from which the client can feel warmth and love when feeling rejected or abandoned. This provides a self soothing resource to manage emotional dysregulation.

Step 5: Then in the outer rung a protective symbol is drawn also repetitively which the client can use to strengthen their boundaries and to provide protection through visualising placing them between themselves and experienced attacking comments/forces in their social life and communications.

Conclusion

In relation to cognitive change, it is obvious that the art therapy field provides a rich and varied array of processes and exercises that facilitate cognitive reappraisal and reframing, distancing, and restructuring which promote emotional self regulation in clients. These exercises are suitable for a wide range of children and adolescents and are particularly appropriate for clients with a trauma background where verbal tools are very limited in their capacity to effect change.

References

Prayoshara (2020) *Mandalas and Modern Psychotherapy* https://www.monkprayogshala.in/blog/2020/1/31/mandalas-and-modern-psychotherapy#:~:text=Mandalas%20are%20also%20used%20in,and%20self%2Dcentring%20by%20some. Accessed 6-3-2023.

Body Dysmorphic Disorder, https://adaa.org/understanding-anxiety/body-dysmorphic-disorder.Accessed 6-3-2023.

Kennert, B., Hartshorne, T., Wanka, A.,Dix ,H., Nicholas, J. (2016) *Self-Regulation of Cognition in CHARGE Syndrome.* https://www.chargesyndrome.org/wp-content/uploads/2016/03/Self_Regulation-of-Cognition-in-CHARGE-Syndrome.pdf

Babouchkina, A., and Robbins, S (2015). Reducing Negative Mood Through Mandala Creation: A Randomized Controlled Trial *Journal of the American Art Therapy Association*. Vol 32, Issue 1, pp34-39.

https://doi.org/10.1080/07421656.2015.994428

Napastek, B.,(2022) Guided *imagery research on mental health.* (https://www.healthjourneys.com/blog/behold-boatloads-of-compelling-guided-imagery-research-on-improving-stress-anxiety-depression-and-qu)

Nguyen ,J., and Brymer, E., (2018) Nature-Based Guided Imagery as an Intervention for State Anxiety. Front Psychol. 2018; 9: 1858. Published online 2018 Oct 2. Doi: 10.3389/fpsyg.2018.01858

Sherwood, P., (2018) *Trauma Informed Structured Sandplay.* Sophia Publications, Western Australia.

Sherwood, P. (2017) *CBT and Artistic Therapies: an Unlikely Marriage.* Sophia Publications, Western Australia.

Sherwood, P (2013) *Emotional Literacy: Adolescent Mental Health.* ACER, Melbourne

Sherwood, P (2009) *Emotional Literacy Workbook.* Sophia Publications, Western Australia

Sherwood, P., (2008) *Emotional Literacy: The Heart of Classroom Management.* Acer, Melbourne

Sherwood, P., (2007) *Holistic Counselling: A New Vision for Mental Health.* Sophia Publications, Western Australia

Sherwood, P., (2004) *The Healing Art of Clay Therapy*, Acer, Melbourne.

Tagar, Y., (1996) *Philophonetics: Love of Sounds,* Melbourne (unpublished)

Tagar, Y., (1998) "Caring for the Child Within" *Philophonetics Love Sounds: language for the inner life*, Vol 2. Persephone publications, Melbourne. pp.53-57.

Pugh, M., 2017 *Pull up a chair* https://www.bps.org.uk/psychologist/pull-chair. Accessed 3/3/23.

Pearson, M., (2000) *Sandplay and Symbol Work: Emotional Healing & Personal Development with Children, Adolescents and Adults*, Acer, Melbourne.

CHAPTER 6

RESPONSE MODULATION

Ref: https://goodtimes.ca/the-power-of-art-therapy/

Emotional Self-Regulation and Artistic Therapies

"Art is my cure to all this madness, sadness and loss of belonging in the world & through it I'll walk myself home."
Nikki Rowe

Introduction

Response modulation refers to efforts to modify an emotional incident once it has occurred usually to repress it if it has a negative quality. This is sometimes referred to as "expressive suppression" and involves stifling the natural behavior expressions of emotion such as laughter, tears, anger, rage, frustration which while appearing to have the short term benefit of emotional self-regulation, in the longer term can have a number deleterious side effects. Franchow and Suchy (2015) show it depletes executive functioning, a finding corroborated by Suchy (2019) with older adults in particular, and Neirmeyer et al. (2019). Goldstein et al. (2013) are particularly critical of expressive suppression as an emotional regulation strategy citing the adverse consequences of this strategy:

> Expressive suppression... can prolong suffering (Carver, Scheier, & Weintraub, 1989; Hayes, Strosahl, & Wilson, 2003), inhibit relationship formation (Butler et al., 2003), impair memory (Richards & Gross, 2000), and have a negative effect on well-being (Chawla &Ostafin, 2007; Gross & John, 2003; John & Gross, 2004). For both children and adults, the suppression of emotion expression does not decrease the psychophysiological experience of that emotion, and may even increase it (Gross & Levenson, 1993, 1997). There are also autonomic costs to expressive suppression. For example, participants who watched a disgusting film

and were instructed to hide their feelings from others showed an increased activation in the sympathetic nervous system (i.e., greater vasoconstriction, greater skin conductance), compared with participants who watched the same film, but were not asked to hide their feelings (Gross, 1998). Long-term use of expressive suppression as an emotion regulation strategy can harmfully affect interpersonal and social functioning (Gross & John, 2003; John & Gross, 2004) and social satisfaction and feelings of connectedness (Srivastava, Tamir, McGonigal, John, & Gross, 2009), decrease overall feelings of positive emotions (Gross & Levenson, 1997) and lower feelings of personal authenticity, and cause higher levels of rumination and possibly depression (Gross & John, 2003). There are indications that children who inhibit their emotional behavior have higher levels of anxiety and depression (Plutchik, 1993) and that children who suppress their anger have higher levels of internalizing symptoms than do children who appropriately express anger (Zeman, Shipman, &Suveg, 2002).

Goldstein etal.(2013) argue that their research indicates that children engaging in drama have higher levels of emotional expression and lower levels of emotional suppression than children who do not.

Here, several techniques and sequences based on dramatherapy will be elucidated to facilitate emotional regulation in children, avert the consequences of expression suppression and provide appropriate forums for the expression of negative emotions. Here are some possible applications that are suitable for groups as well as individuals.

Emotional Self-Regulation and Artistic Therapies

1. Three polarities of feeling in drama.
2. Council of problem explorers.
3. Masks: two faces of x.
4. Emotional doll game.
5. Freeze photo "selfie".
6. Exhaustion relief sequence.
7. Reversal: removing criticism and betrayal.

This is only a small selection of the possibilities offered by dramatherapy.

Dramatherapy sequences for to facilitate emotional expression and promote self-regulation.

1. **Three polarities of feeling in drama (individual, couple or group activity)**

   Assist the child or adolescent to become familiar with the three polarities that govern the expression of feeling and which are illustrated below:

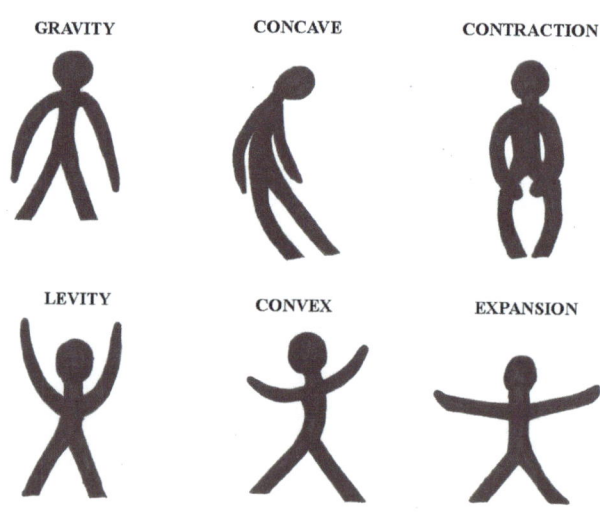

Gravity represents the downward motion when we feel weighed down by the world, too many problems, feeling depressed. Levity represents when we feel elated, joyful, active and jubilant in the world. Concave represents low self-esteem, collapsing inwards with self judgment, despair, hopelessness and lack of self confidence. Convex represents outwardness in the world, becoming full of oneself as one approaches the world. The contraction gesture holds emotions like collapsing boundaries, detachment, isolation, aloneness, numbness in relation to the world and others while expansion represents connectedness, reaching out to friends, activities and engaging in life.

The client completes the following steps:
- Identifies which gestures/posture of the above they find themselves most commonly being.
- Enlarges the negative gestures by walking around the room in one gesture at a time making a correlation between the gesture and their feelings.
- Encourage the client to walk in the opposite polarity to the negative polarity and notice how their feelings begin to change.
- Engage in this technique whenever feeling trapped in a negative polarity until they feel balance between the two polarities.
- Balance occurs when both polarities have been fully expressed.

2. **Council of problem explorers. (group activity)**

   Whenever there is heightened discontent among students, particularly adolescents around a certain issue, this council of problem solvers provides a safe environment for negative feelings to be fully expressed. It also empowers the students to find a way to solve the presenting problem.

Step 1:
- Identify the players in relation to the problem. Give them names. For example, if the problem is use of IT, then identify players like

Facebook, Google, Snapchat, Messenger, Twitter, concerned parent, teacher, adolescent failing at school, adolescent succeeding at school, adolescent with controlling parents, IT addicted adolescent, and so on.
- Invite the members of the group to select one of the above characters to play in the drama.

Step 2:
- Ask the participants to create a mask representing the particular character they have chosen.
- It is easiest to purchase blank masks and have participants alter and/or decorate.

Step 3:
- Participants now start the dialogue and act out their respective character. As a facilitator it is important to ensure all participants have a say.
- Encourage participants to express their feelings positive and negative.

Step 4:
- Move the expression of feelings and ideas towards a meeting place or resolution of the issue if this is possible with this group.
- Debrief all participants upon completion by having them all stand in a circle, take off masks, step backwards and shake their hands vigorously and breathe out any aspect of their role that they feel is still within them.

3. **Masks: two faces of x (individual or group activity)**
   This is particularly suitable for the development of self-awareness of emotional choices in any particular emotionally triggering situation.

Step 1:
- Identify feelings of anger, fear, retreat, rejection or criticism experienced in any particular situation which triggers emotional dysregulation.
- Gesture those feelings and make a mask to represent those feelings.
- Wear the mask.
- Speak those feelings out loud.
- Gesture the feeling after the dysregulating encounter.

Step 2:
- Identify how one would like to feel differently in face of the trigger situation.
- Make a mask representing that positive feeling of peace, calmness, happiness, balance.
- Gesture the positive feelings.
- Wear the mask representing these feelings.
- Speak out loud what could have been said in the situation to avoid emotional dysregulation (Counselor to help here if necessary).

Step 3:
- Identify through the two masks, the two response choices that the client has in a triggering situation.
- Work therapeutically with whatever the client feels is blocking them making the positive choice.

4. **Emotional doll game (pair activity)**
   This dramatherapy technique facilitates the expression of burdensome emotions that underlie emotional dysregulation as well as promoting empathy. It is completed in pairs and adapted from Dayton (1990, pp.116-117).

Emotional Self-Regulation and Artistic Therapies

Step 1
- Have the student select a partner to work with or allocate an appropriate partner.
- Student A then asks student B to guess what they are feeling inside by allowing A to place B's body in the gesture of A's feelings.
- Student B becomes the floppy doll and this enables student A to place the limbs and body of Student B in a gesture that represents how student A is feeling.
- Student B then senses into these bodily gestures and identifies how student A is feeling from the gestures.
- Once student B has guessed correctly, they swap roles and repeat the steps above in reversed roles.

Step 2:
- This time student B places Student A who is acting the floppy doll into the gesture of how they are feeling. It is the reverse of the above.
- Student A is required to identify the correct feeling of student B from the gesture they are experiencing in their body.

Step 3:
- Debrief both students at the end of the game.
- Ask what they now understand more clearly about how their partner was/is feeling.
  This dramatherapy sequence is most helpful in facilitating insight by the students into their emotional life, and in so doing facilitates the identification and empathetic understanding of emotions.

5. **Freeze photo "selfie"**
   This facilitates expression of negative emotion in a safe space so it then curtails the expression of negative emotions in the

social space and inappropriate places. It also enables the client to explore graphically what they actually look like to others when they are emotionally dysregulated and to explore how they would like to look when they are emotionally in control in the situation.

Step 1:
- Recall a social situation in which you experienced emotional outburst.
- Gesture the feeling at the time of the outburst.

Step 2:
- Take a "selfie" of the gesture.
- Now reflect on how that would have looked to others in the social situation.
- Note how you feel NOW reviewing the situation.

Step 3:
- How would you like to have reacted differently in that situation.
- Gesture how you would like to react on the next occasion.

Step 4:
- Take a "selfie" of the gesture
- Ask what you need to do differently on the next occasion to maintain the new gesture of calmness in that social situation.
  This exercise is a very powerful self awareness exercise which facilitates the client gaining insight into the triggering situation, so that in future encounters they are much more aware of their choices and how they appear to the persons around them when they are emotionally dysregulated. Adolescents respond particularly well to this exercise.

6. **Exhaustion relief sequence**

   It is very challenging to maintain emotional regulation when one is exhausted and lacking in rest. Today lack of sleep is a major problem among children and adolescents. Krizan and Hisler, (2018) conclude from their research that: "Sleep restriction universally intensified anger, reversing adaptation trends in which anger diminished with repeated exposure to noise".

   The following exhaustion relief sequence adapted from a conversation with Tagar (1997) is most helpful in skilling a client to notice their exhaustion and undertake an intervention that can be self-directed to restore energy. Hence they should become capable of a more balanced response to an impending social situation in which they are prone to emotional dysregulation.

Step 1:
- Stand up and sense where in your body you feel the centre of the exhaustion. Rate your exhaustion on a scale of 1 to 10 with 10 being maximum exhaustion and 5 being half exhausted. Two is slightly exhausted only. Eight is majorly exhausted. Seven is very significantly exhausted.
- Enlarge the feeling of heaviness and tiredness so that it overtakes the whole body as it spreads from the centre outwards running down your arm and legs and flooding your head, torso and thighs.
- Allow your body to slowly sink into the feeling exhaustion by bending your head, slouching, doubling over and finally collapsing onto the ground as the exhaustion takes over the whole body.

Step 2:
- Once on the ground lie down as if in bed and allow the feeling of exhaustion to flood your whole body.
- Notice how tired you feel and the flooding feeling of the exhaustion through your whole body.

- Take three deep breaths while lying on the ground.

Step 3:
- Sense into your body and name the quality you need to gain some energy (exclude sleep here). Is it quietness, food, water, warmth, happiness, joy, exercise, friendship, a breathing space from performance pressure, and so on.
- Now visualize receiving that quality either from a person who has an abundance of it or from the situation around you.
- Breathe that quality into your body slowly. First breathe it into your torso and head.
- As it moves through your torso gradually sit up slowly.

Step 4:
- Now feel the named quality moving down through your arms and stretch your arms upwards.
- Now feel the same quality moving down through your legs to the tips of your toes and gradually stand upright.
- Once upright start swaying your body from side to side and/or start twisting or rocking in a motion which represents energy moving through your body again.
- Start shaking your hands and feet one at a time. As you shake each part, imagine you are literally shaking off the exhaustion and renewing your energy with the named quality.
- Now move your body in whatever way you feel is comfortable then walk around the room.

Step 5:
- Now access the missing quality if needed such as food or water or a quiet space.
- Rate your exhaustion out of 10 again.

Emotional Self-Regulation and Artistic Therapies

- The level of exhaustion should have decreased markedly if the intervention was effective.

  As a consequence of this intervention, the client should be in a better position to maintain emotional equilibrium in situations that are emotionally triggering for the client and which promote dysregulation.

7. **Reversal; removing criticism and betrayal**

   This is an important dramatherapy exercise that teaches the client how to debrief after emotional dysregulation and return to a balanced centered position as well as develop awareness of the need to maintain their personal space boundary if they are to maintain emotional regulation. Ask the client to do the following.

   Step 1: Place your hand on the part of your body where you feel the betraying or criticising energy has entered into your body which is where you we feel the stress, tension or contracted breathing.

   Step 2: Sense whether the betrayal or criticism feels like a bullet in the back, a punch in the stomach, a kick in the stomach, a dagger in the back, a knife in the heart, a twisted knot in your stomach, an arrow in your heart, a rain of bullets on your head, a bunch of arrows in your heart, or some other force.

   Step 3: Make the sound of the gesture of the force attacking you, for example "ghh..khhh..", and so on. Is it repetitive or a one off? Attacking forces are usually represented by contractions in sounds and consequently one experiences contraction in breathing. Most often they are combinations of consonants because in making consonants we have to contract the flow of the breathing.

   Step 4: Pull out the betraying or criticising energy with your hands making sounds from closed to open that reverse the attacking sound, for example "grrrr to arhhh" as you gesture pulling out the dagger or the knife or untwisting the knot. You are unblocking your contracted breathing so as you push or pull out the attacking force and end with a vowel sound as vowels support open flowing breathing again.

Step 5: Throw the bad energy away and burn it up with a fire sound like "sssssh" so that it disappears.

Step 6: Repeat steps 1-5 until no betraying energy is felt any more in any part of the body.

Step 7: Breathe strength and/or trust back into your body by using a colour which you breathe into your body and a gesture.

Step 7: Surround your personal space with the" d, d, d" dome outlined on pages 25.

Step 8: Breathe deeply and fill your protective dome with your breath which represents protecting your personal space. Become aware that when your personal space if breached, you contract your breathing and then become vulnerable to emotional dysregulation. This exercise, by increasing the flow of the breath through the body, enables the client to be more present to the triggering situation and less reactive. They are more able to make skilful choices as the vibration pattern of energy behind the word/gestures of those they encounter has now been identified, removed and a strong boundary placed around the client. This strengthens their capacity not to be triggered again by that situation or person around similar incidents.

Conclusion

Drama therapy can be seen as a process for restoring mental health and managing behaviours. While it borrows several techniques from theatre. It also employs techniques drawn from cognitive behavioural therapy such a rehearsal, which enable the client to avoid emotional suppression with all its negative consequences for mental health and instead to process negative emotions in a safe space. This space facilities not only the expression of the emotion but also provides a medium for identification of the problem emotion, insight into its activity in the social arena and most importantly offers the client strategies to mitigate emotional dysregulation in the future. As such it is a central artistic therapy in the healthy processing of negative emotions and in the avoidance of emotional dysregulation.

References

Franchow, E.I., & Suchy, Y. (2015). Naturally-occurring expressive suppression in daily life depletes executive functioning. *Emotion, 15(1), 78-89.*

Dayton, t., (1990) *Drama Games: techniques f or self-development.* Innerlook, N.Y.

Suchy, Y. *Niermeyer, M., Franchow, E., Ziemnik, R.* (2019). The deleterious impact of expressive suppression on test performance persists at one-year follow-up in community-dwelling older adults. *The Journal of the International Neuropsychological Society, 25(1), 29-38.*

Niermeyer, M., Ziemnik, R., Franchow, E., Barron, C., Suchy, Y. (2019). Greater Naturally Occurring Expressive Suppression is Associated with Poorer Executive Functioning and Motor Sequence Learning Among Older Adults. *Journal of Clinical and Experimental Neuropsychology, 41(2), 118-132.*

Goldsten, T., Tamar, T., and Winner, l., (2013) Expressive suppression and Acting classes. Psychology of Aesthetics, Creativity, and the Arts © 2012 *American Psychological Association* 2013, Vol. 7, No. 2, 191–196 1931-3896/13/ DOI: 10.1037/a0030209

Krizan, Z., and Hisler, G., (2018) General Manuscript version of Sleepy Anger: Restricted Sleep Amplifies Angry Feelings *Journal of Experimental Psychology.*

https://psycnet.apa.org/manuscript/2018-52927-001.pdf

DOI: https://dx.doi.org/10.1037/xge0000522 Accessed 9/3/2023

CHAPTER 7

CONCLUSION

Ref: https://www.desmoinesregister.com/story/opinion/editorials/2019/02/21/dont-add-more-governmenhttps-pt-red-tape-licensing-art-therapists-massage-therapy-legislature-jobs/2911425002/

Emotional Self-Regulation and Artistic Therapies

"Art gives a feeling of joy and boosts a good mood. Artwork fosters the feeling of relaxation, creativity, and inspiration.

Any form of creativity can reduce the stress hormone cortisol and encourage the good hormones endorphins and dopamine in our brains.

https://italmoda.us/how-does-original-artwork-affects-your-mood-and-your-room/#:~:text=Art%20gives%20a%20feeling%20of,and%20dopamine%20in%20our%20brains. *Acessed 10/3/23*

Conclusion

Emotional self-regulation is a critical life skill affecting our self-management, our social relationships, our capacity to take responsibility for our actions and our ability to function skillfully in our families, communities and the workplace. However, it is important to note that there is not one formula for emotional self-regulation and the precise nature of acceptable emotional self-regulation is culturally defined so that for example Italians will express emotions more freely than English based cultures and expressions, tones, volumes and/or gestures that may be offensive in an English culture, may be regarded as normative in an Italian culture.

Emotional self-regulation is also less challenging for certain character types. So, for example, introverts are more likely to implode emotions and appear more self regulated than extroverts who outwardly are demonstrative with their feelings. However, as pointed out by Van De Kolk (2015, p.98-99) disappearing, numbing out and having no show of emotions are unhealthy signs of a traumatic background and experiences in the individual:

> Trauma has shut their inner compass and robbed them of the imagination they need to create something better. ... the price for ignoring or distorting the body's messages is being unable to detect what is truly dangerous or harmful for you and just as bad, what is safe or nourishing, self-regulation depends on have a friendly relationship with your body. Without it you have to rely on external regulation from medication, drugs like alcohol, constant reassurance or compulsive compliance with the wishes of others.

Most children and adolescents who fail to self-regulate emotions consistently either by violent outbursts or numbing out are victims of trauma. Hence the cost of this failure is pervasive including: few sustained if any friendships, social ostracism, poor academic performance, low self esteem, poor communication and negotiation skills, low levels of self management, poor choices and an inability to communicate their needs clearly and in a socially acceptable style. This means that self governance and growth into adulthood is also constrained and often derailed. Mental health issues and imprisonment for offences compound the problems of many of these children and adolescents in adulthood.

Van De Kolk (2015) recommends the necessity for somatically based interventions to facilitate the development of emotional self-regulation particularly in traumatised clients and this embraces the artistic therapies, a selection of which have been provided in this book. Artistic therapies are particularly effective because most of the sequences presented herein address a number of the emotional self-regulation strategies simultaneously, although for purposes of explication have been grouped under particular strategies.

Emotional Self-Regulation and Artistic Therapies

Situation selection presented basic sequences drawn from dramatherapy including building a safety dome, grounding, learning to sense emotions arising in different parts of the body and strengthening one's self awareness through the eleven directions. All aimed at creating greater bodily awareness of the emotional environment within the client so the client could assess their vulnerability to particular triggers in their social environment, and make skilful choices on whether or not to engage in a particular situation.

Situation modification was addressed through artistic therapies based on sandplay as well as a sequence drawn from clay therapy which focused upon developing a guard. Dramatherapy techniques are always powerful in retraining the body. Rehearsal, speaking up, and the enter exit behold sequences are explored to facilitate the client's bodily sensing of the external environment, and on that basis make appropriate choices including speaking up for one's needs and exiting a situation which the client experiences as overwhelming.

Attentional deployment in emotional self-regulation was explored and focused primarily on artistic therapies drawn from colour and painting work. These included sequences based upon internal resourcing from despair to hope, betrayal to trust and learning how to enlarge positive resources that strengthen the ability to manage emotionally triggering situations.

In relation to cognitive change rather than focusing purely on talk therapy, a range of artistic strategies drawn primarily from colour therapy, clay therapy dramatherapy and sandtray were employed to develop greater self-regulation. The compassion triangle sequence, the empty chair dialogue and family of origin in clay facilitated cognitive reappraisal and reframing, while sandplay and the clay based empathy sequence facilitated distancing.

Distancing particularly involved the drama therapy sequences of boundaries, exiting, staging and empathy creation together with mask making. Guided imagery used sequences drawn from clay therapy and colour therapy including the grief and loss sequence, and the resource mandala.

Response modulation avoids repressing emotional content but rather provides means for expressing it in safe therapeutic environments through a range of dramatherapy techniques which include the three polarities of feeling in drama, Council of problem explorers, Masks: two faces of x, Emotional doll game, Freeze photo "selfie", Exhaustion relief sequence and Reversal: removing criticism and betrayal. These also provide rehearsal opportunities to practice appropriate emotional self-regulation.

Among this plethora of artistic therapy exercises that are somatically based, one must choose the artistic medium that is suitable for a particular client given their individual needs and preferences. The recommendation is to expose oneself to the range of artistic therapies, so that one is able to draw on the wealth of somatically based art therapy sequences to facilitate emotional regulation particularly in clients that have trauma backgrounds and which almost always are those with the highest need for assistance with emotional self-regulation. Hopefully this book will have inspired you to further explore the potential of the somatically based artistic therapies that can provide the bridge between that which is known and can be spoken and that which is stored in the body, unspoken, without words and which runs the show from below the floor boards of consciousness. It is through the bodily awareness that art therapies cultivate, that children and adolescents become aware of their deepest feelings and so can learn to express and manage them in skillful, positive ways and avoid the costs of emotional dysregulation.

Emotional Self-Regulation and Artistic Therapies

Somatic Art Therapy uses movement and body awareness, mindfulness, ritual and art making – drawing, painting, clay, assemblage, collage – to help heal by accessing the pictures we hold about ourselves and our body. When we image our beliefs and attitudes, we can work to change them, allowing for resolution and recovery.https://art-2-heart.com/what-we-do/somatic-arts-therapy/. Accessed 10/3/2023)

www.ingramcontent.com/pod-product-compliance
Lightning Source LLC
Chambersburg PA
CBHW042050290426
44110CB00001B/10